THE SALARIED INDIAN

The untold story of the taxpayers who keep India running

Ajaya K Jena

notionpress.com

INDIA • SINGAPORE • MALAYSIA

This book is not about tax.

It is about the person who pays it.

Gets up every morning.

Works without being asked twice.

Contributes without being thanked once.

This book is for you.

The Salaried Indian.

The untold story of the Taxpayers who keep India running.

Dedicated to

My Parents

Mr. Pramod Jena & Mrs. Babita Jena

My Sister

Miss Prachi Prava Jena

My constant support and strength

Mrs. Samajna Samal

All my friends and colleagues

whose support, feedback, and belief made this book possible.

Special mention

Mr. Puneet Sharma

My mentor, guide, and the inspiration behind every page.

— and —

Every Salaried Indian.

You built this country.

This book is your Thank You.

Contents

Author's Note

I still remember the month my first salary got credited.

I was excited. I had earned it. And then I saw the number — the actual number that hit my account — and felt a quiet, specific confusion. It was less than I expected. Meaningfully less. I scrolled up and found the line. TDS. A number I had not agreed to, had not been asked about, and could not argue with.

I did not feel patriotic in that moment. I felt robbed.

I suspect you have felt that too. If you are salaried, if you have ever stood at that TDS column and felt the same quiet sting — this book was written from that exact feeling. Not to celebrate it. To understand it.

Because here is what I eventually learned, working in finance, watching money move through businesses and balance sheets and budgets: that deduction was not robbery. It was an investment. A stake. A shareholder's contribution to the only India that will ever exist in our lifetime.

I wrote this book as a taxpayer first and a finance professional second. I wrote it because nobody had written the thank-you note that every salaried Indian deserves — and because I believed that if we understood what we were actually paying for, we would carry our salary slip differently.

I am a first-time author. This book is my honest attempt, not a perfect one. If you find something that could be clearer, sharper, or more useful — I genuinely want to hear it. Good feedback is rarer than good intentions, and I will be grateful for both.

Pay with Pride.

– Ajaya K Jena

Chapter 1
The Invisible Heroes

Meet the Man Who Funds a Nation — and Goes Unnoticed

1. THE LAST WORKING DAY

Every month, on the last working day, Ramesh's phone buzzes in his pocket. He is standing in a crowded Mumbai local train, balanced precariously between a door that will not shut and a commuter leaning heavily on his shoulder. The humid air is thick with the smell of rain and struggle. He does not need to look at the screen to know what the notification says. It is the SMS from his bank.

"Salary Credited."

But as he scrolls down his salary slip on the small, cracked screen, his thumb lingers on a specific line: TDS (Tax Deducted at Source). That number — let us say it is Rs. 12,500 — is not just a digital entry. To Ramesh, that number is a language of sacrifice.

What Rs. 12,500 per Month Could Have Been	What It Actually Became
The Kashmir trip promised to his wife	A TDS entry on a salary slip
The sunburst guitar — a buried childhood dream	A contribution to the national treasury
Coaching classes for Priya's (his Daughter) entrance exams	Infrastructure. Defence. Welfare.
Medicine for his father's heart condition	Fuel for a country of 1.4 billion people
The family's emergency safety net	**Gone before it ever touched his palm**

2. THE SILENT CONTRACT

Ramesh realises he is living under a Silent Contract with the government — a contract he never signed and to which no one ever asked for his consent. There was no negotiation. He simply joined a job, worked hard, and found that the state had already decided to be his senior partner, taking its share before he could even provide for his own. It is an automated relationship: join a job, get a salary, pay tax. No questions asked. No consent given.

His day-to-day life is a testament to this silent endurance. His work is boring, stressful, and demands a hectic schedule that leaves him drained. He spends ten hours a day under flickering tube lights, navigating spreadsheets and office politics, often working late into the night. His back aches, his eyes burn from the screen, and the mental load is heavy. Yet he carries out his duties with full dignity. He does not complain; he does not cut corners. He fulfils his end of the bargain with a quiet, steely resolve that the world often mistakes for weakness.

Ramesh looks out the window at the passing city. He sees gleaming glass towers on one side and sprawling shantytowns on the other. He sees a government hoarding celebrating a new billion-dollar expressway. He looks down at his own worn-out shoes and the pothole the train just rattled over.

He feels a strange, quiet tug-of-war in his chest. It is not the loud, burning anger of a rebel. It is something colder — the realisation that he is paying for a VIP seat in a stadium where he is still standing in the general queue.

3. THE ARITHMETIC OF INEQUALITY — THE NARROW FUNNEL

To understand Ramesh's quiet sigh, we have to look at the numbers that haunt the Indian middle class. In a nation of 1.4 billion people, the burden of running the country falls on an incredibly small set of shoulders. According to recent tax filing data, only about 8.2 crore people filed Income Tax Returns in the last assessment year. Out of those, a significant portion falls into the zero-tax bracket after exemptions.

The reality is stark: less than 3 percent of India's population actually pays personal income tax. Ramesh is part of that 3 percent. He is part of the Narrow Funnel through which the dreams of the other 97 percent are filtered. While the government celebrates a record Rs.

19.58 lakh crore in gross Direct Tax collections, Ramesh feels the squeeze.

The Small Giant — Individual vs. Corporate

There is a massive shift happening that the headlines often miss. For the second year in a row, Personal Income Tax collections are projected to exceed Corporate Tax collections. Think about the weight of that. Ramesh is small — one man with one salary slip. The corporations are giants with thousands of employees and billions in revenue. Yet the collective Ramesh of India are now providing more fuel to the national engine than the massive conglomerates.

While big corporations have armies of tax consultants to find every deduction and depreciation loophole, Ramesh has nowhere to hide. He is a Small Giant — more essential to the budget than the biggest names on the stock exchange, yet possessing none of their influence.

4. THE HEROISM OF NO CHOICE

Critics often dismiss Ramesh's contribution. They say: he is not a hero. He pays because he has no choice. His employer deducts it. He cannot hide it.

But this is a cynical view. Ramesh's heroism lies in his integrity within the system. India operates largely on a Shadow Economy. Estimates suggest that India's informal sector still accounts for nearly 40 to 45 percent of the GDP.

Ramesh sees this Shadow Economy every day in his friend Khanna, the shopkeeper. Khanna lives a life Ramesh can only imagine. He drives a big luxury SUV, lives in a sprawling multi-storey house, and his children attend the most expensive international school in the city. Yet Khanna pays zero income tax. He deals in cash, hides his margins, and claims he is just getting by on paper.

Ramesh lives in the Sunlight Economy. Every rupee he earns is tracked. He accepts the transparency of the formal world, even though he knows he is carrying a heavier load than the shadow millionaires like Khanna. He is a hero because, in a land of Jugaad — shortcuts — he chooses the straight path. He is the Moral Anchor of the economy.

5. THE TORTURE OF THE COMPLIANT

The ultimate sting for Ramesh is the torture he faces after paying. He pays for a world-class nation but often receives third-class service.

What He Pays For	What He Receives	The Gap
World-class public hospitals	Long queues, broken equipment, absent doctors	He pays again at a private hospital
Road infrastructure	Deadly potholes that risk his vehicle and his life	He absorbs the damage silently
Efficient public administration	Inspector Raj — treated like a suspect	He navigates the maze alone

He is not a rebel about this. He does not take to the streets. He absorbs it — month after month, year after year — with the quiet, unglamorous dignity of a man who has decided that doing the right thing matters even when the system does not reciprocate.

6. THE SOVEREIGN BUILDER

If India were a massive corporation, the taxpayer would be its primary shareholder. However, in the grand narrative of our nation, the shareholder is treated like a guest who was not invited to the party.

Yet there is a silver lining. Every time Ramesh sees a new Vande Bharat train speed past, a new airport terminal gleaming in the sun, or a massive six-lane highway cutting through the heart of the country, he must realise: he built that.

His tax money is the concrete in those roads. It is the steel in those rails. It is the fuel for the rockets at ISRO. He is not just a passenger — he is the architect of Indian development. He is the reason the country can dream of becoming a ten trillion dollar economy.

The Missing Thank You

When a billionaire donates Rs. 100 crore to a charity, it makes the front page. When a politician inaugurates a project, their face is on every billboard from Kanyakumari to Kashmir. But when Ramesh pays his annual tax, there is no billboard. There is no Thank You note from the Ministry of Finance. Instead, there is often the anxiety of a technical glitch on the e-filing portal.

This book is that missing Thank You.

We need to stop looking at taxpayers as sources of revenue and start seeing them as the Backbone of the Republic. When you see a soldier standing guard, remember that Ramesh bought his boots. When you see a child in a village eating a mid-day meal, remember that Ramesh provided the grain.

7. IT IS TIME TO GIVE THE SHAREHOLDER HIS DUE

Ramesh is not just a salaried employee. He is the silent engine of a nuclear-armed, space-faring, global economy. He is the man who shows up every month, absorbs the deduction without drama, and keeps the lights on for 1.4 billion people — most of whom will never know his name.

It is time we recognised that without the Invisible Heroes, the Indian Dream would have no floor to stand on. It is time the shareholder received the recognition — and the accountability — he has earned.

This is Ramesh's story. But it is also the story of his daughter Priya, who will one day stand at a salary slip of her own; his younger brother Akash, who earns more and resents it; his friend Vikram, who chose honesty and is paying the price; and a woman named Preethi, whom Ramesh has never met, whose choices mirror his own in ways neither of them yet understands.

He is not a victim of this system. He is its primary funder. And a primary funder is not a subject receiving whatever the state decides to distribute. A primary funder is a shareholder.

The chapters that follow will show you what that means — what it costs, what it builds, what it demands, and what it earns. By the end, Ramesh's Rs. 12,500 will not look like a loss. It will look like an investment. And you will know exactly what it bought.

— ❖ —

Chapter 2
The "Bas Chal Raha Hai" Trap

THE COMFORT OF THE CEILING

On Sunday mornings, Ramesh rarely set an alarm. After five days of rushing against time, he allowed himself this small luxury. He would wake up when sunlight entered through the thin curtains and the sounds of the neighborhood slowly replaced silence: a vegetable vendor's call, a pressure cooker's whistle, children laughing in the corridor, and a distant temple bell.

Life felt unhurried. He sat near the window with his cup of tea, watching the city breathe. These were the moments when he thought the most — about his life, and the life of his neighbor, Suresh.

Suresh, the "happiest man on the third floor," had lived next door for almost ten years. Same flat. Same furniture. Same scooter. Same job. They had met when both moved into the building as young, hopeful men. But over time, their paths separated. Suresh had held the same administrative desk job for twelve years. He arrives home at 5:30 PM sharp, waters his balcony plants, and spends his evenings watching news debates with a plate of biscuits.

One Sunday, Suresh joined Ramesh on the balcony.

"Office ka kya scene hai?" (How's work?) he asked.

"Busy as usual," Ramesh replied. "And you?"

Suresh shrugged with that tranquil smile. "Same. But at least no tension. Bas, chal raha hai." (It's just going on.)

To Suresh, this is a badge of spiritual honor. It signifies "Santosh" (contentment). He believes he has escaped the "rat race." But if you look at Suresh's bank balance and the inflation charts of the last decade, a different story emerges. Suresh's "peace" is actually a calculated retreat. By staying in a low-risk, low-growth bubble, he ensures he never has to face a challenge — but he also ensures he never increases his capacity to contribute to the nation.

For Suresh, "enough" has quietly become a ceiling.

But here is what Suresh never thinks about on that balcony: his stillness is not free. It has a price — and that price is paid by Ramesh.

Every month, when Ramesh opens his salary slip and sees ₹12,500 disappearing as TDS before it even touches his palm, a portion of that deduction exists precisely because Suresh has chosen to contribute nothing. The government has a fixed budget to run the country — roads, hospitals, defense, schools. That budget must be collected from somewhere. When millions of Suresh opt out of the formal economy, the entire weight of that budget falls on the narrow shoulders of the Rameshs. Suresh's "peace" is, in brutal economic terms, a tax on Ramesh's ambition.

Think of it this way: if Suresh were earning ₹30,000 a month and contributing even a modest ₹1,200 in direct and indirect taxes, and if a million Suresh across India did the same, the treasury would gain ₹1,200 crore every month. That is enough to hire **thousands of doctors** for government hospitals, lay kilometers of rural roads, or fund scholarships for children who have no other path forward. Instead, that money simply does not exist. And Ramesh makes up the difference.

Suresh is not just standing still. He is — unknowingly, perhaps without malice — standing on Ramesh's shoulders.

CHILDHOOD LESSONS AND THE FEAR OF RISK

Ramesh remembered his school days in a small town. Teachers often asked: "Beta, bada hoke kya banoge?" (What will you become?) Most answers were the same: Clerk, Teacher, Policeman, or a Bank job. Safe jobs. Respectable jobs. Jobs with pensions. No one said Scientist, Entrepreneur, Designer, or Researcher. Dreams were filtered early by fear.

His parents, meaning well, had always emphasized security. "Risk mat lena" (Don't take risks). "Naukri chhodna mat" (Don't leave your job). They had lived through uncertainty and poverty; for them, safety was survival. But as Ramesh looked at Suresh, he realized that safety had slowly become the only goal, and that goal was a trap.

THE MACRO-COST OF MICRO-AMBITION

In India, we have romanticized "simplicity" to a fault. But there is a cold financial reality behind this mindset. When a million Sureshes decide that "good enough is enough," the national engine begins to sputter.

Economists often talk about the "Middle-Income Trap." This is a stage where a country's growth plateaus because its citizens stop innovating and start seeking "rent" — living off what they already have rather than creating new value. This mindset directly stops the nation in its tracks.

When millions settle for low-productivity roles, the government faces a chronic lack of funds. This leads to fewer railway lines being laid to connect rural markets. It means specialized hospital tests remain unavailable or unaffordable in public clinics because the state cannot afford the latest technology. Infrastructure projects stall, and the quality of public life stagnates because the collective contribution is too low to fuel high-speed development.

THE PRODUCTIVITY GAP AND "HIGHER HOPE"

Consider the GVA (Gross Value Added) per worker. If our per-capita GDP is to move from the current ~$2,700 toward the $10,000 mark needed for "Developed Nation" status, we cannot have a population satisfied with "just getting by."

When Ramesh pushes for a promotion or a new skill, he is moving up the "Value Chain." High ambition is the fuel for "Higher Hope." A person with higher hope doesn't just want a bigger salary; they believe in a future where they can solve bigger problems, build bigger businesses, and provide a better standard of living for their community. Ambition is the psychological engine of a country's progress. Without it, we are just managing poverty rather than creating wealth.

THE "INFORMAL" SECURITY BLANKET AND THE SHADOW ECONOMY

The "Bas Chal Raha Hai" mindset is the parent of the Informal Economy. Currently, nearly 90% of India's workforce is in the informal sector. These are the people who stay "small" to stay under the tax radar.

The Shadow Economy is fueled by this avoidance: the boutique owner who only accepts UPI payments to a personal mobile number to hide turnover; the freelancer who asks for "cash" in exchange for a discount; the contractor who pays laborers in cash to avoid provident fund contributions; the real estate agent who deals in "black money" to help a client "save" on stamp duty.

They stay informal because it feels safe. But this freedom is fragile. Ramesh saw this in his cousin Meena. When her husband fell sick, they realized they had no insurance, no savings, and — crucially — no credit history. Because years of "cash income" had left them invisible to banks, they couldn't get a loan. Low ambition protected them from tax, but it did not protect them from life. By avoiding the system, they disqualified themselves from the National Infrastructure of Credit and Security.

MEDIOCRITY AS A SOCIAL SHIELD

In our social circles, we often use "family time" or "peace of mind" as a shield to hide our fear of the Responsibility of Success. High income in India is a spotlight. It means a 30% tax bracket, more compliance, and being a "stakeholder" who has to care about how the country is run.

For Suresh, staying small is a way to stay "innocent." If he doesn't earn much, he doesn't owe much. He can sit on his balcony and complain about the government for hours without ever having to feel "skin in the game." He is a consumer of the nation, but not a builder of it.

Let us put hard numbers to this invisible injustice. Consider two men living in the same building, using the same roads, breathing the same city air, protected by the same police force, and served by the same public infrastructure.

Ramesh earns ₹1,50,000 a month. After TDS and GST on his consumption, he contributes approximately **₹40,000 to ₹45,000 per month** to the national treasury — through direct income tax, GST on the branded goods he buys, fuel tax, and insurance.

Suresh earns ₹30,000 a month. He pays zero income tax. He buys mostly unbranded essentials taxed at 5% GST. His total monthly contribution to the national treasury is approximately **₹1,200**.

Ramesh is contributing over thirty times more than Suresh to the nation that both of them equally inhabit and consume. Both men walk on the same flyover. Both men's children breathe air kept clean by the same environmental programs. Both men sleep behind the security of the same defense budget. But only one of them is paying for it with any meaningful weight.

This is not just unfair. It is the foundational economic injustice of the Indian middle class — a quiet, invisible, structural robbery that nobody talks about at dinner parties. And yet it shapes every rupee Ramesh earns, every deduction on his salary slip, and every EMI that squeezes his monthly budget.

THE STAGNATION OF A NATION: DIVIDEND VS. DISASTER

India is currently enjoying a "Demographic Dividend," with a median age of 28. But a dividend is only a benefit if it is invested. If the youth adopts Suresh's philosophy of "seeking shelter" instead of "seeking growth," we will face a "Demographic Disaster."

Ramesh meets his college friends once a year. One friend, Amit, said quietly, "I wanted to start something, but… too risky now." At 35, he was too young to give up, but too tired to try.

When energy stays unused because competition is scary and comfort is easy, the burden of the entire nation shifts onto the few who do strive.

India's Demographic Dividend is not a permanent gift. It is a ticking clock. By approximately 2040, India's population will begin to age. The ratio of working citizens to dependent citizens will start to narrow. The window within which a large, young, ambitious workforce can build the hospitals, roads, pension systems, and institutions needed to support an older India is roughly 15 years long.

Every year that a Suresh spends in comfortable stagnation is a year stolen from that window. The tragedy is not simply that Suresh is not contributing today. The tragedy is that the infrastructure he refuses to help fund today is the very infrastructure that will need to carry him when he is 65 and no longer earning. He is, quite literally, undermining his own future by being "comfortable" in his present.

A nation cannot afford the luxury of an entire generation that settles for less — not when time is the one resource that cannot be recovered.

A CALL TO DISCOMFORT

We must stop asking, "How much is enough for me?" and start asking, "What is my maximum potential?" Being an ambitious Indian is not about buying a bigger car; it is about increasing your weight in the Republic. The more you grow, the more you earn, and the more you contribute, the more moral authority you have to demand a better India.

That night, Ramesh looked at his daughter sleeping. He made a silent promise: He would teach her to be brave. To try, to fail, and to grow. He would teach her that there is dignity in simple living, but there is danger in stopped dreaming.

Peace is a beautiful thing, but it should be the reward at the end of a productive life, not a hiding spot in the middle of it. The next time someone tells you, "Bas, chal raha hai," remind them: A nation that stands still is actually falling behind.

Before you close this chapter, ask yourself one honest question: Are you a Ramesh or a Suresh?

Not in terms of income — income is not the measure. The measure is intention. Are you pushing against your ceiling, or have you quietly decided that the ceiling is the sky? Are you contributing your full weight to the Republic, or are you consuming its infrastructure while leaving the bill for someone else?

The "Bas Chal Raha Hai" trap is seductive precisely because it doesn't feel like a trap. It feels like wisdom. It feels like peace. It even feels, sometimes, like spirituality. But when you place Suresh's contentment next to Ramesh's salary slip — when you see the deduction, feel the squeeze, and understand who is paying for whom — the philosophy loses its halo.

Contentment is peace. But **ambition is responsibility.** And in a developing nation with a closing demographic window, a struggling tax base, and 1.4 billion people counting on each other, responsibility is not optional.

A growing citizen builds a growing nation. A stagnant citizen — however peaceful, however "spiritual" — is a weight the nation carries silently, one rupee of Ramesh's TDS at a time.

— ❖ —

Chapter 3
The ROI of Citizenship

Where Does Your Tax Money Actually Go?

Ramesh is sitting at his dining table, helping his daughter Priya with her geography project. They are looking at a map of India — a vast tapestry dotted with ports, power plants, and industrial corridors. Priya's crayon traces a new highway line, and she asks: "Papa, who builds all of this?"

Ramesh looks at his tax challan from the previous year, neatly filed in a folder. He does the math in his head. I paid enough tax last year to buy a high-end motorcycle, he thinks. A machine I could see, touch, and ride. Instead, that money is gone. I don't see my name on a single brick in this city. Where is the receipt for my contribution?

In India, there is a deeply ingrained belief that tax money falls into a "black hole" of corruption and bureaucratic waste. While leakages are a real and frustrating part of the system, this Black Hole theory is often used as a psychological excuse to devalue our own contribution. To find the receipt, Ramesh needs to look at the macro-assets that allow his micro-life to function. He needs to understand that his tax is not a fee he pays to a stranger — it is the equity he holds in his own home.

1. THE PANDEMIC — WHEN THE SYSTEM WAS PUT TO THE TEST

Ramesh first became truly curious about taxes during the pandemic. Before that, they were just numbers on a screen — deductions, percentages, forms, and deadlines — handled once a year and forgotten.

In March 2020, his office closed suddenly. One evening, his manager announced on a video call: "From tomorrow, work from home." No one knew what that meant. Streets became empty. Shops shut down. Trains stopped. Hospitals filled. Fear spread faster than the virus.

Ramesh watched the news every night: ambulances, overcrowded wards, doctors in protective suits, and oxygen shortages. Then came the announcements — free treatment, free vaccines, relief packages, special trains, and massive food distribution.

One night, while scrolling through the news, Ramesh paused. "How is the government managing this?" he wondered. Hospitals were expanding overnight, vaccines were being produced by the billions, and millions of stranded workers were being transported home. Nothing was cheap.

He suddenly remembered his salary slip. The income tax he had paid every month for years. A connection formed in his mind. This was where it went.

The Pre-Paid Safety Net

The COVID-19 pandemic provided a brutal, high-stakes lesson in the ROI of citizenship. During the height of the crisis, the Indian government launched the Pradhan

Mantri Garib Kalyan Anna Yojana, providing free food grains to over 80 crore people. At the same time, the national vaccination drive delivered over 220 crore doses.

To the person standing in the clinic, the vaccine was "free." But as a taxpayer, Ramesh knew better: it wasn't free. It was pre-paid. His tax was the insurance premium he had been paying for years. When the Black Swan event arrived, that collective pool of capital was the only thing standing between the nation and total collapse. The ROI wasn't a profit in his bank account — it was the fact that the economy didn't stop breathing.

From a Deduction to a Hospital Bed

Later that year, the reality hit home. His uncle fell ill. They rushed him to a government hospital. Ramesh had always avoided such hospitals before, fearing long queues, slow service, and overworked staff. But this time, he saw something different: new equipment, digital records, and better facilities.

It wasn't perfect, but it was improving. A nurse helped his uncle patiently. A doctor explained the situation calmly. Outside, people waited quietly. No payment was demanded. No bribe was asked. For the first time, Ramesh felt a swell of quiet pride. He looked at the gleaming diagnostic machines and thought: My money is here.

2. THE FLYOVER AND THE DIGITAL RUPEE — INFRASTRUCTURE YOU USE EVERY DAY

When Ramesh switches on a light bulb, he doesn't see the Rs. 2.5 Lakh Crore the government spends annually on power and renewable energy subsidies. When he uses a public flyover to shave 20 minutes off his commute, he is using a piece of the Rs. 11.11 Lakh Crore allocated for Capital Expenditure in the 2024-25 budget.

Every morning, Ramesh crosses the same flyover. Years ago, that road had been narrow and broken. Traffic jams were routine — people wasted hours of their lives in the heat. During construction, people complained: "Waste of money. Why here? Nothing will change." But when it opened, travel time plummeted and accidents fell. Now, no one remembers the complaints. They only enjoy the benefit.

Then there is the Digital ROI. Every time Ramesh uses a UPI app to pay a street vendor, he is standing on a digital public good called the India Stack. While other countries struggle with expensive private banking transaction fees, India's digital payment infrastructure — funded and secured by the state — processed over 131 billion transactions in the last fiscal year. For Ramesh, the cost of his tax is visible in the fact that he doesn't have to carry a thick wallet of cash or worry about the security of his digital identity. In most countries, that infrastructure is owned by Visa or Mastercard, and it costs a percentage of every transaction. In India, it was built with public money. His money.

THE SCHOOL VISIT

One day, Priya brought home a brochure. Her school had received new smart boards and digital classroom resources under a government programme. Ramesh attended the orientation. The principal spoke proudly: "These facilities are possible because of government support."

Government support. Ramesh translated that in his mind: public money. Taxpayers. Me. He saw the children interacting with global resources on those screens and realised that his Kashmir trip money was being transformed into the knowledge of the next generation. It was a legacy he was building — brick by digital brick.

The Railway Journey

Every Diwali, Ramesh travelled to his hometown by train. He loved watching the villages pass by — the fields, the rivers, the stations. The railways were not perfect; platforms were crowded and trains were sometimes late. But they connected 1.4 billion people.

From Kashmir to Kanyakumari, the railways provided subsidised tickets and mass transport that no private company could run alone at those prices. It ran on public money. It was the physical manifestation of a shared national identity — and Ramesh was a silent financier of every kilometre of track.

3. THE SILENT SERVICES — WHAT YOU NEVER NOTICE UNTIL THEY'RE GONE

Ramesh started noticing the Invisible ROI in small things. The streetlights that worked at night, providing safety for his wife when she returned from work. Garbage collection every morning that prevented the spread of disease. Water supply pipelines reaching into the newest suburbs. The public park where his father took his evening walks.

And then the less visible layer: the courts and the police. Without a funded judiciary and police force, there would be chaos. Even if a court case is slow, the existence of the law is a barrier against anarchy. Ramesh can sign a contract, buy a flat, dispute a bill, and know that if someone cheats him, there is a mechanism — imperfect, slow, but real — that he can use. That mechanism was built by public money. His money.

Defence — The Expensive Price of Peace

During border tensions, news channels were full of debates about missiles, jets, and surveillance. Ramesh imagined the cost: equipment, training, logistics, housing. Protecting a country of 1.4 billion people is incredibly expensive. The Defence Budget stands at over Rs. 6.21 Lakh Crore.

This money ensures that Ramesh can argue about tax rates in a coffee shop rather than worry about an invading force. He realised that his tax was, in a very literal sense, the security guard at his door.

Welfare — Supporting the Weakest

Once, Ramesh volunteered with an NGO to distribute ration kits in a slum area. He saw families who depended entirely on government schemes: free food, housing support, and pensions. He realised that without taxes, these people would be left behind. The weakest would suffer first. Taxes were not just about infrastructure — they were about the moral fibre of a society that refuses to let its most vulnerable perish.

Why Borrowing Is Not the Answer

A friend once said: "Why doesn't the government just take loans instead of taxing us so much?" Ramesh thought about it. Loans have interest. Future generations would pay for today's comfort. Debt was delayed pain; taxes were shared responsibility. One was easy today; the other was fair always. By paying now, he was ensuring his daughter would not be born into a debt-trap nation.

4. THE DOUBLE ENGINE — HOW AMBITION FUNDS THE NATION TWICE

Ramesh realised that the story didn't end with income tax. There is a hidden link between ambition and indirect tax that most people overlook. When a person stays in the Bas Chal Raha Hai comfort zone, their consumption stays flat. They buy the bare essentials, most of which fall in the zero or 5 percent GST bracket.

But when Ramesh is ambitious — when he works that hectic job to earn a higher salary — his lifestyle evolves. This evolution is not just luxury. It is a massive increase in his contribution to the national treasury through GST. Because Ramesh strives for a better life, he buys a laptop for Priya's coding classes at 18 percent GST. He buys a mid-sized car to take his parents to the hospital in comfort at 28 percent GST plus cess. He takes his family to an AC restaurant to celebrate a promotion at 18 percent GST. Every time Ramesh upgrades his life through hard work, he becomes a Double Engine for India.

Engine One: he pays a higher percentage of his income as Direct Tax. Engine Two: he pays a higher volume of Indirect Tax because his ambitious lifestyle touches premium GST slabs. The same man, taxed twice — visibly and invisibly — simply because he chose to grow.

The Direct vs. Indirect Tax Distinction

Income Tax is a Direct Tax — it reflects one's ability to contribute. While everyone pays GST on food and clothes, Income Tax is the premium paid by those who have succeeded within the system. It is a more powerful reflection of a citizen's stake in the country. It is the difference between being a casual visitor and a permanent resident.

5. THE NUMBERS — RAMESH AND SURESH, SIDE BY SIDE

To see the Double Engine clearly, compare Ramesh — the ambitious taxpayer — with his neighbour Suresh, who has settled for the comfort zone.

Category	Suresh (Stagnant)	Ramesh (Ambitious)	What It Means
Monthly Income	Rs. 30,000	Rs. 1,50,000	Ramesh earns 5x more
Direct Tax (TDS)	Rs. 0	Rs. 22,500 (~15% effective)	Suresh contributes nothing direct
Avg. GST Rate	5% (essentials)	18–28% (services & comforts)	Ramesh's lifestyle touches premium slabs

Monthly GST Paid	~Rs. 1,200	~Rs. 18,000	15x more in indirect tax alone
Total Monthly Contribution	**Rs. 1,200**	**Rs. 40,500**	Ramesh carries 33x more weight

Ramesh is not contributing 5 or 10 times more than Suresh. Because of his ambition and his higher spending capacity, he is contributing over 33 times more to the nation's survival every single month. While Suresh thinks he is being simple and spiritual by not wanting more, the math shows that he is providing very little fuel for the hospitals and roads he equally uses. Ramesh, by being ambitious, is carrying thirty-three Sureshes on his back.

6. THE SHADOW VS. THE SUNLIGHT — WHY HIDING INCOME POISONS BOTH ENGINES

This is why the Shadow Economy is so damaging. When a wealthy shopkeeper hides his income, he might pay some GST on his luxury purchases, but he completely chokes the First Engine — Direct Tax. He enjoys the landlord's lifestyle while paying tenant rates.

Ramesh, standing in the sunlight of the formal economy, pays at both ends. His ambition is transparent. He cannot hide his success, so he cannot hide his contribution. This gives him the ultimate sovereign right to ask: If I am the one providing the fuel for both engines, why am I still the one navigating the potholes?

Ambition in India is not a private affair. It is a national service. Every time a citizen dreams bigger, earns more, and spends more, they are literally building a brick of future India. The Invisible Hero is the person who refuses to stay small — because they know that a small life leads to a small nation.

7. FROM "THEIR MONEY" TO "MY ASSETS" — THE SHIFT THAT CHANGES EVERYTHING

The critical shift in mindset is moving from being a payer to being an owner. If you bought a luxury apartment and found the elevator broken, you wouldn't just complain — you would demand a fix, because it is your property. By recognising that he is a primary funder of the Rs. 48 Lakh Crore national budget, Ramesh gains the moral authority to demand quality.

o evades tax is a tenant: they live in the country but have no stake in its upkeep. A citizen who pays tax is a landlord: the roads, the schools, and the satellites belong to them. Not as a metaphor. As a structural reality. The landlord does not ask permission to call the plumber. The landlord calls the plumber.

The Journey of One Rupee

Ramesh imagined his one rupee leaving his salary slip and travelling through the vast bureaucratic pipes of the nation. He saw it being split across the three great demands of the state.

Budget Head	Amount Allocated	What It Means to Ramesh
Capital Expenditure (Infrastructure)	Rs. 11.11 Lakh Crore	The flyover, the highway, the metro
Defence	Rs. 6.21 Lakh Crore	The soldier at the border
Interest Payments	~Rs. 11 Lakh Crore	Cost of past borrowing — paid by Ramesh

That one rupee multiplied into impact. It became a brick in a bridge, a vial of medicine, a bullet in a soldier's rifle, and a meal in a hungry child's bowl. It was not lost. It was transformed.

8. THE SILENT DIVIDEND — CLOSING THE NOTEBOOK

Ramesh will never get a thank-you call from the Prime Minister. But every time a new Vande Bharat train cuts travel time, or a village gets its first tap-water connection under the Jal Jeevan Mission — which has reached over 75 percent of rural households — Ramesh is receiving a dividend.

He is the silent partner in every Indian success story. His receipt is not a piece of paper. It is the fact that he lives in a country that is building, not just surviving.

Next time you walk on a road, sit in a train, or visit a hospital — ask yourself: Who paid for this? You know the answer. Your tax is not lost. It is transformed. Into services. Into security. Into opportunity. Into India.

And when you pay honestly, you are not losing money. You are investing in a nation.

— ❖ —

Chapter 4

Growth Brings Responsibility

Why the High Earner Owes the Most — and Gets the Most

The rainy season in Bengaluru has a way of turning the city's high-tech corridors into a shimmering, neon-lit gridlock. Ramesh's younger brother, Akash, represents the absolute vanguard of the new, ambitious India. At 29, he is a Lead Product Manager for a high-growth fintech startup headquartered in HSR Layout.

Akash does not just work — he sprints. He works 14-hour days, often fuelled by lukewarm coffee and the adrenaline of a looming Series C funding round. He eats lunch at his desk — usually a quick bowl of salad ordered through an app — and for him, weekends have long since ceased to be days of rest. They are merely extended workdays where he catches up on strategic documentation he could not finish during the week's frantic meetings.

One Tuesday evening, after the annual performance bonuses were credited, Akash called Ramesh. He was not calling to celebrate his hard-earned success. He was calling to vent a frustration that had been simmering for years.

"Bhaiya, I'm looking at my payslip, and it feels like a punch to the gut," Akash started, his voice crackling over the Bluetooth in his car as he sat in the infamous Silk Board traffic. "Look at this deduction — Rs. 4.5 Lakhs gone in a single year just from the bonus and the monthly TDS. That's not just a number; that's a down payment on a car! That's a luxury watch I wanted to buy for Mom! Why am I being punished for working hard? I'm the one sacrificing sleep. The government is my 30 percent business partner when I win, but where are they when I burn out? Where is the Burnout Subsidy?"

Akash's frustration is the anthem of the rising Indian upper-middle class. It is the cry of the professional who feels they are being milked to sustain a system that gives them nothing in return. In India, as soon as you cross the threshold of comfort — roughly Rs. 15 to 20 Lakhs per annum — you hit a psychological wall. You stop feeling like a beneficiary of the state and start feeling like its victim. You begin to see the Tax Department not as a collector of resources for the common good, but as a predator on your personal ambition.

This feeling is valid. But it is also dangerous. It stems from a fundamental misunderstanding of what we call the Ecosystem of Wealth.

1. THE MYTH OF THE SELF-MADE MAN

In the startup world, we love the story of the self-made man. We worship the coder who studied under streetlights, the entrepreneur who started in a dusty garage, and the executive who rose from a small town. But if we peel back the layers and look through a macroeconomic lens, the concept of being self-made is a convenient lie.

Wealth is not created in a vacuum. It is grown in soil that has been fertilised for decades by public spending, collective security, and state-funded innovation. To help Akash understand why he owes the 30 percent, we have to dissect the very platform he stands on.

The Digital Rails — The India Stack

Akash's fintech company does not handle physical cash. It moves billions of rupees digitally. This company exists — and Akash has a high-paying job — only because the government built the India Stack: Aadhaar, UPI, and e-KYC.

In developed nations like the USA, a company doing what Akash's does would have to pay 2 to 3 percent in transaction fees to private giants like Visa or Mastercard. In India, the government created a digital public highway that is essentially free for the user. Without this taxpayer-funded public good, his company's customer acquisition cost would be 10 times higher. The business model would likely collapse — and Akash's bonus would never have existed in the first place.

The Legal Floor and the Security Net

Contracts are enforceable — mostly — because of the judiciary. If a client defaults or a partner tries to steal the startup's intellectual property, Akash has legal recourse. We take this for granted, but in a failed state with no tax revenue, business is conducted with private militias and protection money, not contracts and courts. The 30 percent tax is, in part, the subscription fee for a society where the rule of law allows Akash to focus on coding rather than guarding his office with a shotgun.

2. THE SUBSIDISED SUCCESS AUDIT — THE DEBT OF HONOUR

Ramesh listened to Akash's rant and then asked a simple question: "Akash, do you remember who paid for your degree?"

"I did, Bhaiya. I had an education loan."

"No," Ramesh replied. "You paid the fees. You didn't pay the cost."

This is a reality check most successful Indians choose to ignore. Akash is a graduate of an elite National Institute of Technology. He feels he got there through pure merit. But merit does not build a 100-acre campus, buy multi-crore laboratory equipment, or pay the salaries of world-class PhD professors.

A typical student at an IIT or NIT pays roughly Rs. 8 to 10 Lakhs in total fees for a four-year degree. However, the actual expenditure by the government to produce one such engineer — including infrastructure, research grants, and administrative overhead — is estimated to be between Rs. 35 Lakhs and Rs. 40 Lakhs. Every time Akash looks at his tax deduction, he needs to realise he is not being robbed. He is slowly paying back a Debt of Honour. He is settling the Rs. 30 Lakh subsidy that the previous generation of taxpayers — people like Ramesh — provided for him when he was just a student with a dream. He was a beneficiary of the state for twenty years. He has only been a contributor for five.

3. THE TRUE PICTURE — THE PUSHERS AND THE PULLERS

To truly understand why the burden feels so heavy on Akash's shoulders, we must look at the full picture of the Indian economy — a vision that goes beyond spreadsheets and into the realm of national psychology.

Imagine a massive, ornate carriage representing the Indian Republic. It is loaded with the dreams, the food security, the healthcare, and the future of 1.4 billion people. On one end, you have the Pushers — the 3 percent of the population who are formal taxpayers. The Rameshs and the Akashes. They have their shoulders against the back of the carriage, muscles screaming, heels digging into the mud, trying to push this massive weight up the hill toward Developed Nation status.

On the other side are the Pullers. The Pullers are not the desperately poor who cannot walk — the system is designed to carry those who truly cannot move. The Pullers are those who have chosen a lazy attitude and a comfort zone. They are the healthy youth who refuse to upskill because things are just going on. They are the shopkeepers who make a profit of Rs. 2 Lakhs a month but refuse to generate a single GST bill. They are the professionals who demand cash payments to keep their income below the tax threshold.

When a million people decide that good enough is enough and retreat into the shadow economy, they are not just staying still. They are pulling the economy down. By refusing to contribute their fair share of fuel, they increase the weight that the Pushers have to carry. Akash's tax is high not just because the government spends money — but because he is carrying the lazy debt of those who refuse to leave their comfort zones. Every time a Puller takes a free vaccine or drives on a highway without contributing a rupee of income tax, Akash is paying for it. Stagnation is not a private luxury. It is a public cost.

4. THE ARITHMETIC OF THE CREAM LAYER

To understand the weight of responsibility, we must look at the Pyramid of Privilege. In the assessment year 2023-24, the Income Tax Department released revealing data. The number of individuals declaring an annual income of over Rs. 1 Crore was roughly 1.69 lakh — just 169,000 people.

Pause and let that number sink in. In a country of 140 Crore people, fewer than 2 Lakh people are in the Crorepati income bracket officially. If you are earning even Rs. 20 Lakhs a year, you are not middle class in the statistical sense. You are in the top 3 to 4 percent of the Indian economy. You are the Cream Layer.

The Bottom 50 percent struggle for daily sustenance — the state must protect them simply so they can survive. The Middle 40 percent struggle for stability — small shopkeepers and farmers who are one bad monsoon away from crisis. The Top 10 percent, where Akash sits, are the only ones with the capacity to struggle for Legacy.

When you are at the top of the pyramid, gravity works differently. You are the structural integrity of the nation. If the top 10 percent decides to opt out or evade, the base cannot support the structure. The Surcharge levied on the super-rich is not a penalty. It is the Stability Premium — the price paid to ensure that inequality does not become so sharp that the entire social fabric tears apart.

5. THE BRAIN DRAIN ARGUMENT — STABILITY VS. OPPORTUNITY

"If they tax me too much, I will just leave," Akash often threatens. "I'll move to Dubai — no income tax. Or London — better parks."

This is the most common threat from the high earner. And the numbers show they are not bluffing. In 2022 alone, roughly 6,500 millionaires were projected to leave India, seeking better quality of life — cleaner air, pothole-free roads, and a system that works.

But there is a critical counter-argument: the Arbitrage of Growth. If Akash moves to London, he will pay 40 to 45 percent tax — significantly higher than India's 30 percent. Yes, he will get better roads. But he will be living in an economy growing at 0.5 to 1 percent. He will be a tiny cog in a giant, old machine. He will never see his company grow 100 percent year on year.

In the West, you pay high tax for Stability — a house that is already built. In India, you pay moderate tax for Opportunity — the right to build the mansion yourself.

India is one of the last great growth stories in human history. The responsibility of the high earner is to stay and fix the plumbing of the nation, not flee to a house built by someone else's ancestors. Leaving India because of the tax is like leaving a startup just before its IPO because the office coffee is bad. You are trading your upside for comfort.

6. THE SOCIAL MATHEMATICS — ONE CARRYING FIFTY

Consider the social footprint of a high earner. Ramesh, earning Rs. 8 Lakhs, pays enough tax to perhaps support one child's education in a government school. Akash, with his Rs. 30 Lakhs income and bonus, pays enough tax to support an entire classroom. This is not a burden. This is Leverage.

Akash often complains that politicians waste his money. But look at where that 30 percent actually goes. It pays the salary of the policeman who ensures Akash can walk to his car at midnight in Bengaluru without fear. It funds the public health centres that prevent a polio or COVID-19 outbreak from reaching his office. It funds the scientists at ISRO who launch the satellites that allow his fintech app to have precise GPS and timing data.

When you earn more, your social footprint expands. You move from being a User of the state to being a Trustee of the state.

Level of Income	Economic Identity	Social Responsibility
Low Income	Dependent	Survival
Middle Income	Partner	Stability & Growth
High Income (Akash)	**Trustee**	**Nation-Building & Stewardship**

As a Trustee, you are not giving away money. You are managing the capital of the Republic to ensure the environment remains conducive for you to make even more money next year.

7. ETHICAL WEALTH VS. PARASITIC WEALTH

Historically, India has had a deep tradition of Ethical Wealth. Business houses like the Tatas did not just build companies — they built entire ecosystems. When they built Jamshedpur, they did not just build a factory. They built schools, hospitals, and parks for people who were not even their employees. They viewed tax and philanthropy not as a loss, but as a Sovereign Duty to the land that gave them resources.

Today, we see a rise in Parasitic Wealth. These are people who extract maximum value from the Indian market — using our roads, our youth's labour, and our digital rails — but store their wealth in offshore tax havens or real estate cash traps. They want the benefits of India but refuse to pay the costs of India.

Akash has a choice. He can be a Parasite — doing everything to minimise his loss to the country, hiding in the shadows of the Pullers. Or he can be a Builder.

> ***"I have succeeded because this country gave me a platform. Now, I must pay the dividend to the 1.4 billion shareholders who allowed me to rise."***

8. THE ULTIMATE ROI — CHAOS INSURANCE

Finally, why should Akash pay? Why should he care about the Pullers or the Bottom 50 percent?

Because inequality is a ticking time bomb. History teaches a brutal lesson: you cannot have a society of glistening islands of billionaires and high-tech startups surrounded by an ocean of desperate poverty forever. Eventually, the ocean rises. If the gap becomes too wide, society collapses into crime, riots, or revolution.

By paying his fair share, Akash is not just funding a road he might never drive on. He is buying Social Stability. He is ensuring that the have-nots get enough support — rations, basic health, and a bridge to the middle class — so that they do not feel the need to tear down the gates of his apartment complex.

Tax is the insurance premium we pay for a peaceful society. It ensures that the ladder we climbed does not get kicked away by the people still standing at the bottom. It ensures that the Pushers can continue to push without being pulled down into the mud by the weight of a collapsing social order.

9. THE TRANSFORMATION — FROM VICTIM TO SOVEREIGN

Ramesh's phone call with Akash ended with a long silence. Akash looked out his window at the streetlights — lights powered by a grid he helped fund, illuminating a road built by his contributions, guarded by a police force he subsidised.

The Rs. 4.5 Lakhs was not gone. It was distributed. It was working. It was the engine oil in the machine that made his life possible.

The next morning, Akash did not go to work feeling like a victim. He went to work feeling like a Sovereign. He was not just a Product Manager. He was a Primary Funder of the Indian Republic. And that realisation gave him a power that no bonus could ever match.

The country you want is the country you pay for. If you want a first-class nation, you must stop resenting the cost of the ticket.

You must lead the charge from the front of the carriage, knowing that while the Pullers may slow you down, your strength is the only thing keeping the nation moving toward the sunlight.

— ❖ —

Chapter 5

The Middle-Class Squeeze

Too Rich for Aid, Too Poor for Comfort

1. THE FIRST SUNDAY OF THE MONTH

It is the first Sunday of the month. The rest of the neighbourhood is asleep, enjoying the quiet hum of a weekend morning. But Ramesh is already awake, carrying the invisible weight of the calendar.

He sits at his small dining table with a calculator and a ruled notebook. The tea in his cup has gone cold. This is his monthly ritual — the Budgeting Hour. Not an hour of wealth management or investment strategy. An hour of survival mathematics.

On one side of the page: his net take-home pay. A fixed, stubborn number that has barely kept pace with the changing world outside his window. On the other side: the Mandatory Outflows.

Monthly Outflow	Amount
Home Loan EMI	**Rs. 35,000**
School Fees (quarterly averaged)	**Rs. 12,000**
Parents Medical Expenses	**Rs. 8,000**
Groceries and Utilities	**Rs. 15,000**

Fuel and Transport	**Rs. 6,000**
SIP (Investments)	**Rs. 10,000**
Total Fixed Outflows	**Rs. 86,000**

He punches the numbers into the calculator with mechanical dread. By the time he reaches the bottom of the page, the Surplus is a dangerously thin number. That tiny remainder is supposed to cover emergencies, weekend outings, clothing, and the occasional dream of a vacation.

He stares at it for a moment. Then he closes the notebook.

He is not poor. He knows this. He earns more than ninety-seven percent of this country. He has a home, a job with benefits, a daughter in a decent school. By every statistical measure, he is doing well.

And yet the number at the bottom of that page does not feel like doing well. It feels like balance — the relentless, exhausting maintenance of a position that can be lost in a single bad month.

2. THE SANDWICH CLASS — CAUGHT IN THE STRUCTURAL VICE

Ramesh belongs to what economists call the Sandwich Class. He is caught in a structural vice grip between two extremes of the Indian socioeconomic spectrum, and the vice is tightening.

Below him: the Low-Income Group, which benefits from the state welfare architecture — free rations under PMGKAY covering 80 crore beneficiaries, housing under PM Awas Yojana, direct cash transfers, free healthcare at public facilities. The state acts as their safety net, and rightly so.

Above him: High-Net-Worth Individuals and large corporates, who benefit from Production Linked Incentives, corporate tax cuts from 30 percent to 22 percent, the ability to hire wealth managers to optimise every rupee of liability, and the leverage to negotiate directly with the economy on their own terms.

Ramesh is in the middle. He is too rich to receive support. Too honest to escape the burden. He falls into the gaping void of policy neglect — paying full market rate for housing, private schooling because public schools are not a reliable option for competitive education, unsubsidised fuel, and private health insurance because public healthcare cannot absorb his family needs at the level they require.

He is the solitary pillar holding up the roof, **receiving neither the shelter of the rich nor the aid of the poor.** He is the most financially reliable citizen in the country and the most institutionally ignored one.

3. THE SILENT KILLER — LIFESTYLE INFLATION VS. WHAT THE GOVERNMENT MEASURES

Government data regularly cites Consumer Price Index inflation at a manageable 5 or 6 percent. News anchors celebrate this as a triumph of economic management. Ramesh reads it in the newspaper and feels gaslit.

If inflation is only 6 percent, why does his life feel 20 percent more expensive than last year?

The answer lies in the gap between headline CPI and what might be called Lifestyle Inflation — the rate at which the actual cost of a middle-class life is rising. The CPI basket is heavily weighted toward food staples and fuel. Ramesh's life is built on entirely different pillars.

Education Inflation

Private school fees and competitive coaching costs have been rising at 10 to 12 percent per annum for the past decade. This is not because schools are becoming dramatically better. It is because the demand for quality English-medium education vastly exceeds the supply of institutions that can credibly deliver it, and because the entrance exam ecosystem has created a parallel industry of coaching that costs more than the schooling itself. To give Priya a fighting chance in a hyper-competitive system, Ramesh has to absorb this hike every year, without a matching hike in his own income.

Medical Inflation

Healthcare costs in India are rising at approximately 14 percent per annum — one of the highest rates in Asia. When his father needs a specialised cardiac test, the 6 percent CPI figure becomes a cruel abstraction. The diagnostic centre does not accept CPI as payment.

When Ramesh's salary hike is 8 percent but his two largest non-negotiable costs — education and health — rise at 10 to 14 percent, he is **effectively getting poorer every year** even as his nominal income climbs. He earns more on paper, gets pushed into a higher tax bracket, and finds his grocery bags lighter and his wallet emptier. This is the Middle-Income Trap at a household level — inflation the data does not capture, imposed on the class that can least afford to absorb it silently.

4. THE DOUBLE ENGINE — HOW RAMESH PAYS TWICE

We often speak of the government Double Engine of growth. But the middle-class salaried professional is the actual double engine funding that growth. He is not taxed once. He is taxed twice — and the second taxation is invisible.

Here is the arithmetic of a single rupee in Ramesh hands. Ramesh earns Rs. 100. Income tax takes Rs. 30, leaving him Rs. 70. This is Engine One — the direct extraction of his labour. Then Ramesh lives his life. He fills fuel for the family scooter: nearly 50 percent of the pump price is central and state tax. He buys a laptop for Priya's coding class: 18 percent GST. He takes his parents to dinner at a mid-range restaurant: 5 percent GST. He pays the health insurance premium: 18 percent GST. He buys an air conditioner for the summer: 28 percent GST. This is Engine Two — the taxation of his consumption, levied after the direct taxation of his income.

By the time Ramesh has earned and spent his salary, the government has effectively recovered 40 to 50 paise of every rupee he made — through a combination of direct and indirect taxes that no single line item on his salary slip fully captures.

Now consider Vicky. Ramesh's cousin. Twenty-four years old, lives in a tier-2 city, operates entirely in the cash economy. Freelance event management. No GST registration. No ITR. **Vicky's effective contribution to the national treasury: close to zero.**

Vicky is not contributing to the engine. He is a passenger. And when Akash looks at his Rs. 4.5 lakh TDS deduction with resentment, and when Ramesh looks at the thin surplus at the bottom of his budget notebook, part of what they are looking at is the mathematical consequence of Vicky's free ride. Every Vicky in India is a hidden surcharge on every Ramesh and every Akash.

5. THE EMOTIONAL COST — ONE CRISIS AWAY

The heaviest load Ramesh carries is not financial. It is psychological.

He knows, with the quiet clarity of a man who has done the arithmetic too many times, that he is One Crisis Away from genuine difficulty. Not poverty in the absolute sense — he has savings, he has assets, he has an ITR history that would get him a loan. But one serious crisis: a job loss in the wrong year, a health emergency not fully covered by insurance, a market correction that wipes out a portion of his SIP corpus at the wrong moment — and the careful structure of his financial life becomes fragile in ways that would take years to repair.

The state that receives his contribution every month provides him no specific protection against this fragility. There is no unemployment insurance for the formally employed salaried class. There is no contributory pension building on his behalf outside of what he arranges himself. There is no mechanism that says: because you paid for thirty years, here is your proportional claim in this moment of need.

He is taxed like a citizen of a European welfare state and protected like a citizen of an unregulated one. He pays the premiums of social democracy and receives the safety net of a frontier economy.

This is the structural paradox that no budget speech addresses. The honest salaried taxpayer is simultaneously the most reliable revenue source in the country and the most underserved citizen in it. His reliability is taken for granted. His vulnerability is ignored.

He runs on a treadmill where the speed keeps increasing and the pause button has been removed.

6. THE SOVEREIGN TRUSTEE — CLOSING THE NOTEBOOK DIFFERENTLY

On this particular Sunday morning, as the neighbourhood begins to wake around him and the cold tea sits forgotten beside the notebook, something shifts in Ramesh.

He has felt the resentment before. The squeeze, the exhaustion, the specific frustration of watching Vicky post travel photos while his own Kashmir trip remains perpetually deferred. He has felt all of it, and it has always resolved into a dull, resigned acceptance.

But this time he looks at the number at the bottom of the page differently. Not at what it represents as a loss — the vacation, the guitar, the upgrade. He looks at what it represents as a contribution.

That thin surplus is not the whole story. The whole story includes the Rs. 86,000 in outflows — of which a substantial portion, through direct and indirect taxes, has already entered the national economy and become something. A brick somewhere. A salary somewhere. A meal somewhere. A chance somewhere. Not efficiently, not without waste, not without the legitimate frustration that accompanies imperfect governance. But real.

Ramesh is not a victim of this system. He is its primary funder. And a primary funder is not a subject receiving whatever the state decides to dispense. A primary funder is a shareholder — with the leverage, the moral authority, and the standing to demand that the investment be managed well.

The Middle-Class Squeeze is real. The double engine burden is real. The one-crisis-away anxiety is real. None of it is imagined or dismissed here. But the response to that reality is not **retreat into the shadow economy** — which makes the squeeze worse for everyone. The response is to stay in the sunlight, contribute fully, and exercise the most powerful right that contribution confers: the right to stand in the room and say, loudly and with evidence, that the system is not delivering what it should.

Ramesh closes his notebook. He is the National Shock Absorber — the elastic centre that takes the pressure and stays standing. Not because the system has earned his loyalty cheaply. But because his loyalty is the only force keeping the structure from collapsing inward.

He is not a hostage to his budget. He is the primary shareholder of a rising Republic.

Pay with Pride. Demand with Power. Build with Passion.

— ❖ —

Chapter 6

The Price of Being Honest

Fear, Notices, and the Compliance Trap

1. THE GHOST AT THE DOOR

It is a Tuesday afternoon, the kind of mundane, humid day where the clock seems to crawl. Ramesh is at his office desk, his mind split between a project deadline and the mental checklist of evening chores — Priya homework, his mother medication, the grocery run he keeps postponing.

His phone vibrates. A sharp, mechanical buzz that cuts through his concentration.

He glances at the screen. It is an email notification.

The sender: CPC-Income Tax Department.

The subject line: Intimation u/s 143(1) of the Income Tax Act, 1961.

In an instant, the atmosphere of the room changes. The air feels thinner. His heart begins a frantic, uneven rhythm. His palms, moments ago dry, are slick with sweat.

Ramesh is an impeccably honest taxpayer. He declares every rupee of savings account interest, every fixed deposit return, every component of his HRA exactly as it is. He has never inflated a claim, hidden an income source, or structured a transaction to reduce his visible earnings. He has nothing to hide.

And yet the fear arrives anyway. It arrives before the email is opened. Before the content is read. Before any evidence of wrongdoing — which does not exist — could possibly be established.

This is the Tax of Anxiety. It is an invisible, unquantified levy that the state extracts from the mental peace of its most loyal citizens. It does not appear on any Form 26AS. It cannot be claimed as a deduction. But it drains the lifeblood of millions of honest Indians every year with the same reliability as TDS.

For Ramesh, that email is not data. It is a ghost at the door. And the ghost arrives specifically because Ramesh has done nothing wrong.

2. THE PERVERSE LOGIC — HONESTY MAKES YOU A TARGET

Ramesh stares at the subject line for a full minute before clicking. In that minute, his mind runs through the familiar labyrinth of worst-case scenarios.

Did he calculate the interest on that old fixed deposit correctly? Did his employer make a data entry error in the TDS filing? Is the system reading the Rs. 50,000 he transferred to his mother as unexplained income?

Each question is answered, internally, with a reasonable explanation. The fear does not fully go away until the email is opened and confirmed as a routine processing intimation — which it is, in this case, as it is in most cases for the genuinely honest filer.

But here is what the honest taxpayer understands that nobody says aloud: the fear is not irrational. It is the logical response to a deeply perverse incentive structure.

If Ramesh were invisible — operating in cash, keeping no formal books, accepting no digital payments — the Income Tax Department would have no email address to send a notice to. No PAN-linked transaction trail to query. **The shadow economy is not just untaxed. It is unreachable.** And the honest taxpayer who stepped into the sunlight, who declared everything, who made himself completely visible — he is the one who receives the notice.

The system punishes the visible to compensate for its inability to reach the invisible. The honest taxpayer discovers that transparency is not protection. It is exposure.

Honesty does not bring confidence in India. It brings vulnerability. The shadows are safe. The sunlight is where the notices arrive.

Ramesh knows this. Every honest taxpayer in India knows this. They stay honest anyway — out of principle, out of the values their parents taught them, out of the quiet conviction that a society functions on the choices people make when no one is watching. But the fear never fully leaves. The system has made it structurally permanent.

3. DAVID VS. THE ALGORITHMIC GOLIATH

The relationship between Ramesh and the Income Tax Department is not one between equals. It is one of the most asymmetric power relationships in the life of an ordinary Indian citizen.

What the Department Has

The Integrated Taxpayer Profile — a comprehensive digital dossier aggregating credit card spends, mutual fund investments, international travel, property transactions, and bank interest across multiple institutions. Project Insight — the AI-powered analytics system that scans for lifestyle mismatches. The power to freeze a bank account with a single digital command. The authority to levy penalties of 200 percent of the disputed tax amount. The power to reopen assessments from up to seven years ago — meaning Ramesh could today be asked to produce a rent receipt from a flat he lived in three jobs and two cities ago.

What Ramesh Has

A PDF reader. A slow government portal that crashes at peak traffic. Limited legal knowledge. A 9-to-5 job that allows no time to visit tax offices. And a deep, ancestral fear of government matters inherited from a system that historically treated the citizen as a suspect until proven compliant.

Ramesh knows the stories. The average time to resolve genuine tax litigation in India is 12 to 15 years. In the bureaucratic arithmetic of this system, the process is the punishment. The department does not need to prove you are guilty. It only needs to keep you inside the system long enough to exhaust your patience, your savings, and your will to fight.

This is why, when faced with a dubious demand for Rs. 10,000, Ramesh — and millions like him — will simply pay it. Not because they owe it. Because Rs. 10,000 is cheaper than the CA fees, the lost working days, the anxiety, and the years of follow-up that contesting it would require. **They are not paying a tax. They are paying protection money to be left alone.**

4. THE LEMON SQUEEZER LOGIC

The Income Tax Department operates under collection targets. Every year, there is a revenue goal, and there are officers and zones accountable for meeting it. This creates a structural pressure that produces a predictable and deeply unjust outcome.

A tax officer under pressure has two choices. First: go into the streets and find the millions of unregistered shopkeepers, cash-only contractors, undisclosed rental earners, and wealthy non-filers. Document their income. Build a case. This requires significant resources, field investigation, and institutional will that a target-driven quarterly review cycle does not naturally produce.

Second: open the database of people who are already filing. They have email addresses. They have PAN numbers. They have digital footprints. Send them a notice. The second option is always easier. And the second option is Ramesh.

It is always easier to squeeze the lemon already in your hand than to climb the tree to find new fruit. The system punishes the visible to compensate for the invisible.

When the metric is revenue collected and the path of least resistance is the already-compliant taxpayer, the already-compliant taxpayer becomes the default target. The more honest Ramesh is, the more detailed his digital trail, the more useful he becomes as a source of incremental collection pressure. His honesty is not protection. It is exposure.

5. THE COMPLIANCE TAX — THE HIDDEN FEE OF INTEGRITY

We talk often about the 30 percent tax bracket. We almost never talk about the additional compliance overhead that honest taxpayers carry on top of it. Being honest is expensive — not just in the rupees paid to the government. Expensive in the hidden costs the formal economy imposes exclusively on the people already inside it.

The CA Fee

Every year, Ramesh pays between Rs. 5,000 and Rs. 10,000 to a Chartered Accountant. He is a well-educated professional. But he is, in the eyes of the old Income Tax Act 819-section labyrinth, functionally illiterate. He is paying not for financial advice. He is paying for a Safety Shield — someone who knows the specific sub-proviso that protects him from the specific notice that his honest but unguided filing might inadvertently trigger.

The Sunday Cost

Three Sundays a year, Ramesh does not rest. He sits in a room littered with bank statements, insurance premium certificates, school fee vouchers, and Form 16s, acting as an unpaid pro-bono auditor for the government. He is performing a service that the department requires of him and for which he receives no compensation, no acknowledgment, and no reduction in the probability of receiving a notice anyway.

While his cash-economy neighbour spends those Sundays at a brunch paid for informally, Ramesh spends them maintaining the documentary proof of his own honesty.

The Cognitive Load

The mental bandwidth consumed by tax compliance is a cost that does not appear on any balance sheet but is real and significant. Every March, millions of the nation most productive professionals stop thinking about the problems they are paid to solve and start thinking about investment proof deadlines, old regime versus new regime calculations, and ELSS statement retrieval. The nation loses billions of productive hours annually to the administration of its own honesty.

6. THE CANTEEN — THE LONELINESS OF THE COMPLIANT

A few days after the Tuesday email — which turned out to be a routine processing intimation, requiring no action, meaning nothing — Ramesh is sitting in his office canteen. The conversation has turned, as it does in canteens across India every other week, to money.

His colleague — a man who earns roughly the same salary as Ramesh but operates a parallel cash consulting business on the side — leans back with the relaxed satisfaction of someone who has recently made a decision he is proud of.

He says: I just bought the new SUV. Registered in my father name — he is technically a farmer on paper. Full depreciation, zero income tax implication. Plus I paid 50 percent in cash directly to the dealer. He wanted it too — saved him the GST. Everyone goes home happy.

The table reacts with warmth. Someone calls him Smart. Someone else calls him a Hustler. The word is affectionate. The tone is admiring.

Ramesh sits quietly. He thinks about his Rs. 12,500 monthly TDS. He thinks about the Tuesday email that made his heart race for twenty minutes even though he had done absolutely nothing wrong. He thinks about the three Sundays spent gathering documents, and the CA fee paid to ensure those documents were assembled correctly, and the thin surplus at the bottom of his budget notebook.

He does not feel smart. He feels like a Sucker.

He feels like the student who studied all night for the ethics exam while everyone else bought the question paper and got an A. He passed. They passed too. The grade is the same. The method was not.

Ramesh stays honest. Not because the system rewards it — it demonstrably does not. Not because society admires it — this canteen is evidence that it does not. He stays honest because his father taught him that integrity is what you do when no one is watching. Because his daughter is watching. Because somewhere in the private accounting of who he is, the cost of the shortcut is higher than its price.

But he wishes — sitting quietly in that canteen, feeling the full loneliness of the compliant — that the government would stop watching him so closely and start watching the people who are actually cheating.

7. THE BRIDGE THAT BENDS BUT DOES NOT BREAK

That evening, Ramesh is at his dining table. The Tuesday email is resolved. The canteen conversation is still sitting with him, not as anger — he has moved past anger — but as a clear-eyed recognition of the cost.

He is the National Shock Absorber. The elastic centre of an economy that has built its revenue model around his reliability. When the system needs money, it finds Ramesh — because his email address is on file, his PAN is linked to everything, and his compliance history makes him the path of least resistance. When the economy tightens, it is Ramesh who adjusts — postpones the vacation, tells Priya maybe next year for the bicycle, absorbs the inflation silently because he has no mechanism to pass it on.

He is a Bridge. This is not a metaphor for comfort — it is a description of structural function. A bridge carries weight. It groans under the pressure of the trucks crossing it. It bears the wind and the rain. It does not complain about the weight. It is designed for the weight. But a bridge that is never maintained, never reinforced — a bridge that is only ever loaded and never strengthened — will eventually fail. And when a bridge fails, the two sides of the river do not meet.

If Ramesh stops being honest — if the honest taxpayers of India collectively decide that the canteen colleague is right, that the smart move is to join the shadow economy — the revenue base does not gradually erode. **It collapses.** There are too few Rameshs carrying too much weight, and there is no redundancy in a system that depends entirely on them.

He is not honest because the system has fully earned it. He is honest because he has decided, in the private accounting of his own character, that he will not be the person who breaks the bridge. That he will not be the reason the two sides of the river cannot meet.

His honesty is not weakness. It is not naivety. It is not the absence of better options. It is the Quiet Strength of the person who understands what the system requires of him and chooses to provide it — not out of compliance, but out of conviction.

He wants his daughter to grow up in a country where success does not require a lie. And that country is built, one honest declaration at a time, by the people who choose it when no one is watching.

The Price of Honesty is high.
The Value of Integrity is infinite.

— ❖ —

Chapter 7

The Stories We Tell Ourselves

The Anatomy of an Excuse — and the Courage to Reject It

1. THE BENGALURU ROOFTOP — A DIFFERENT KIND OF CANTEEN

It is a Thursday evening in Bengaluru. The kind of evening where the city's air finally cools after a brutal afternoon, and the tech parks of Whitefield glow like a constellation of glass and ambition from the rooftop of a mid-rise apartment complex.

Ramesh is visiting his younger brother Arjun for the weekend. At a rooftop gathering of Arjun's colleagues — a casual post-sprint Friday-eve unwinding that somehow happened on a Thursday — Ramesh finds himself standing next to Preethi.

Preethi is 32. Senior Manager, Product Engineering, at one of Bengaluru's fastest-scaling IT product companies. She is the kind of person who commands a room without trying to — not because she is loud, but because when she speaks, the quality of what she says makes people instinctively pay attention. She has a direct, analytical gaze, the kind earned through years of being the only woman in a room full of people who assumed she got there by accident.

She didn't. She got there by being twice as good, working twice as hard, and refusing twice as many shortcuts.

Ramesh knows of her through Arjun — knows that she negotiated her own salary hike from twelve lakhs to twenty-two in two years without a single advocate in her corner. Knows that she bought her own apartment at 30, a 2-BHK in HSR Layout, carrying her education loan EMI and the home loan EMI simultaneously for eight months until the education loan closed. Knows that she sends a fixed amount home to her parents in Coimbatore every month without fail, and that she has never once spoken about it as a sacrifice.

She is, by any honest measure, exactly the kind of citizen this country needs more of.

Which is why what she says next surprises Ramesh enough to stay with him for weeks.

2. THE CONFESSION THAT WASN'T

They are talking about the new tax filing portal — the one that crashed spectacularly for three consecutive years during peak filing season — and Preethi says it with the calm, matter-of-fact tone of someone stating a known law of physics:

"I declare everything from my salary. The TDS is automatic anyway, I have no choice. But the rent I collect from my flatmate? That goes into a separate account. I don't declare it. I know I should. I just... don't. The system has taken enough from me already. It can't have this too."

She says it without guilt. Without lowering her voice. Not as a boast — more as a simple statement of a private equation she has made with herself and is entirely at peace with.

Around her, two or three people nod. Someone says "same, honestly." Someone else laughs in recognition.

Ramesh doesn't say anything in that moment. He smiles, nods, takes a sip of his chai, and watches the city lights below.

But inside, something shifts. Because Ramesh recognizes in Preethi's words something he has felt himself — many times, at many moments, over many years of watching his TDS column grow while the pothole outside his building refused to get fixed. He has felt the same pull. The same temptation to draw a private line and say: this far and no further. The system gets my salary. It doesn't get everything.

The difference is that Ramesh never crossed that line. And tonight, quietly, in his own mind, he wants to understand why. Not to judge Preethi — he respects her enormously. But to examine, honestly, the arguments she made. Because they are not her arguments alone. They are the arguments of millions of honest, intelligent, hardworking Indians who have quietly decided that one small act of personal exemption is justified.

He wants to understand the architecture of that justification. Because only by understanding it fully can he know whether it holds.

3. THE INTERNAL AUDIT — RAMESH SITS WITH THE EXCUSES

That night, on the fold-out bed in Arjun's spare room, Ramesh cannot sleep. The city hums below. His mind runs through Preethi's words again, and then — with the kind of honesty that only comes at midnight when no one is watching — he runs through his own.

He has heard these arguments before. He has felt them before. He decides to take each one seriously. To give it its full weight. To see if it stands.

He thinks of them as the Six Fortresses. The walls that intelligent, decent people build around their private decisions to not fully contribute. Each fortress looks solid from the outside. Each one, he decides, must be examined from the inside.

Excuse#1	**The Corruption Fallacy** *"The government will only waste it or steal it anyway."*

This is the oldest fortress. The most emotionally satisfying. Preethi didn't say it tonight — she is too analytical for such a blunt argument — but Ramesh has heard it from a hundred others, and he has felt its pull himself. When he watches a news report about a collapsed bridge that was inaugurated six months ago, there is a moment — just a moment — where the thought forms: why am I funding this?

He sits with it. He gives it full respect.

And then he does the arithmetic that the argument refuses to do.

Yes, there is leakage in the system. Yes, there is corruption. India's governance record is imperfect — deeply so in many areas. But the argument that corruption justifies non-contribution is not a moral position. It is a mathematical one. And the mathematics does not work.

India's Tax-to-GDP ratio is approximately 11%. The OECD average — the club of developed nations India aspires to join — is approximately 34%. The gap between what India collects and what it needs is not primarily caused by corruption at the top. It is caused by the vast, distributed, individual decisions of millions of Preethi-level earners to quietly exempt some portion of their income from the formal record.

If every intelligent professional who used "corruption" as their justification instead contributed honestly, the aggregate change in national revenue would dwarf the amount lost to even the most headline-grabbing scams. The scams are visible and infuriating. The distributed micro-evasion is invisible and catastrophic.

More fundamentally: the logic creates a **self-fulfilling prophecy of failure.** We don't pay because the service is poor. Because we don't pay, the government has less to spend on maintaining and improving the service. The service remains poor. We use the poor service to justify paying even less next year. The cycle tightens. The system gets exactly as broken as we collectively decide it deserves to be — and then we complain about the breakage.

A country is not a vending machine where you insert coins only when the machine works perfectly. It is a construction site. You contribute to build it. The building is imperfect. You contribute to improve it. The alternative is not a better vending machine. The alternative is no building at all.

Fortress One does not hold.

Excuse#2	**The ROI Blindness** *"I buy all my services privately. What exactly am I paying the government for?"*

This is Preethi's argument, stated more precisely. She pays for her own internet, her own health insurance, her own building security, her own inverter for power cuts. She has, effectively, privatized her entire lifestyle. So she asks — genuinely, analytically, without malice — what the state provides that she is actually consuming.

Ramesh understands the logic. He has lived it. But he also knows what the logic misses.

It misses the Invisible Infrastructure — the vast, unglamorous, foundational layer of national life that makes Preethi's entire existence possible and that no private company could ever replicate.

Her IT company exists because contracts are legally enforceable. If a client defaults on a ten-crore payment, Preethi's company does not send a private army. It sends a legal notice, backed by a judiciary funded by public money. Without that legal floor, business is conducted with intimidation, not contracts. Her salary — her twenty-two lakhs, her negotiated hike, her financial independence — is denominated in a currency whose value is maintained by the Reserve Bank of India, a public institution. Without a stable rupee, every number on her payslip becomes meaningless.

Her fintech apps work because India built UPI — a taxpayer-funded digital public highway that processes over 130 billion transactions a year at near-zero cost to the user. In any other country, that infrastructure would be owned by Visa or Mastercard, taking 2-3% of every transaction. In India, it was built by the state, for free, for everyone, including Preethi.

She travels safely between Mumbai and Bengaluru because the Indian Air Force and Navy maintain the security perimeter that keeps the skies and seas around this country stable enough for commercial aviation to exist. She does not pay for that security in a line item she can see. She pays for it in taxes — or she is supposed to.

The ROI of citizenship is not visible in any single transaction. It is the **sum of all transactions being possible at all.** Tax is not a purchase of a specific service. It is a subscription fee for the existence of a functioning society — the invisible platform on which every private purchase, every career achievement, and every act of personal financial independence rests.

Fortress Two does not hold.

Excuse#3	**The Drop in the Ocean** *"I'm just one person. My rental income won't make a difference."*

This is the most seductive fortress because it feels humble. It positions non-contribution not as selfishness but as realism. What is Preethi's undeclared rent — perhaps twenty thousand rupees a month — in a national budget measured in lakh crore?

Ramesh thinks about this carefully. And then he does what the argument deliberately avoids: he multiplies.

India has approximately 2.2 crore individuals who actually pay meaningful income tax after all deductions.

Of these, a very conservative estimate suggests that at least 30 to 40 percent have some form of undisclosed supplementary income — rental income, freelance payments, cash consulting fees, interest from informal loans. If each of these individuals is hiding an average of just fifteen thousand rupees a month in undeclared income, the annual aggregate is in the range of one lakh crore rupees or more.

One lakh crore rupees. That is the entire annual budget of several state governments combined. That is enough to staff and equip hundreds of new government hospitals. That is enough to eliminate the deficit in India's primary education teacher shortage. That is enough, if deployed as capital expenditure, to build infrastructure that would generate economic returns for decades.

Preethi's "drop" is not a drop. It is one molecule in an ocean of identical drops, each one separately convinced of its own insignificance, collectively constituting a catastrophic deficit.

The "I am just one person" argument is only ever made by people who have forgotten that **every systemic problem is the sum of individual decisions.** Traffic jams are not caused by one car. Pollution is not caused by one factory. The tax gap is not caused by one undeclared rent. They are each caused by millions of individuals separately concluding that their personal contribution to the problem is too small to matter.

Fortress Three does not hold.

Excuse#4	**The Victim Mentality** *"I already pay so much. I have earned the right to protect this little bit."*

This one is the most personal for Ramesh. Because it is the one he has felt most acutely. He understands it not as an abstraction but as a lived emotion — the physical sensation of watching ₹12,500 disappear from his salary before it reaches his account, month after month, year after year, while the pothole outside his building sits untouched.

He understands Preethi's version of this even more viscerally. She has paid for everything herself, always. Her education, her apartment, her parents' security, her own career advancement — all of it without subsidy, without support, without a system that ever leaned in her direction. She arrived at her senior manager title despite the system, not because of it. The idea that the same system now wants a share of the additional income she generates from an asset she bought with her own money, in her own name, through her own effort — this is experienced not as civic duty but as insult.

Ramesh respects this feeling deeply. It is real. It is earned.

But he also knows that feelings, however valid, are not arguments. And the feeling of victimhood — however justified in its origin — can quietly become the permission slip for choices that compound the very problem causing the original grievance.

The honest taxpayer is not a victim. The honest taxpayer is a **sovereign.** The difference is not semantic — it is the entire psychological architecture of citizenship. A victim pays tax and feels robbed. A sovereign pays tax and feels empowered — because the sovereign understands that contribution is the source of the moral authority to demand accountability. The more you pay, the louder your right to demand that the money be used well. Stepping back from contribution does not protect you from the system's failures. It simply removes your standing to fight them.

Preethi has fought every battle of her life from the front. She did not step back from her salary negotiation because the company's HR system was imperfect. She did not step back from her home loan because the banking system was complicated. She fought, she demanded, she won. The tax system deserves the same energy — not retreat.

Fortress Four does not hold.

Excuse#5	**The Passive Optimist** *"India is growing at 7% anyway. The system will fix itself without my small contribution."*

This is the newest fortress. The one that belongs specifically to the generation Preethi represents — the analytically minded, data-literate, growth-optimistic Indian professional in their thirties who follows GDP charts and startup funding rounds and genuinely believes that India's economic trajectory is strong enough to absorb individual non-compliance.

It is the most sophisticated excuse and therefore the most dangerous one.

Because it is partially true. India is growing. The formal economy is expanding. Digital infrastructure is deepening. Tax collections are hitting record highs. On the surface, the machine appears to be working fine without everyone's full contribution.

But the 7% GDP growth figure conceals a brutal internal inequality of effort. That growth is being driven by a very small proportion of the population — the Rameshs, the Akashes, the formal-sector professionals — who are contributing at full weight. The growth rate would be dramatically higher if the broader population contributed at their actual capacity. India's potential growth rate, if its tax base matched even 60% of OECD levels, is not 7%. It is closer to 9 or 10%. The difference between 7% and 9% compounded over twenty years is not a rounding error — it is the difference between a developing nation and a developed one.

The "system will fix itself" argument is the economic equivalent of **free-riding on someone else's effort** and calling it optimism. India is growing not because non-contributors are giving it space to breathe. It is growing because contributors are working hard enough to compensate for the non-contributors. The optimist who points at the growth chart and says "see, we don't need my contribution" is essentially pointing at the rowers in the boat and saying "see, the boat is moving fine." The boat is moving. The rowers are exhausted. And the passenger is calling it proof that rowing wasn't necessary.

Fortress Five does not hold.

Excuse#6	**The Generous Soul**

"I give more than I take. My parents, my siblings, the people I quietly fund — that money does more good in my hands than in the government's."

This is the sixth fortress. And it is the one Ramesh almost does not want to examine — because unlike the other five, it is not built on resentment or laziness or cynicism. It is built on something genuinely admirable: love.

Preethi did not say this at the rooftop. But Ramesh knows the people who do. He has heard it from his cousin who supports two younger siblings through college and sends money home to ageing parents in a village with no pension system. He has heard it from the doctor who runs a free Saturday clinic in a slum colony and feels, entirely reasonably, that the six hours she gives every week are worth more to real human lives than the additional few thousand rupees the government would collect in tax on her consulting income. He has heard it from the NGO founder who channels every discretionary rupee into a cause he built with his own hands and can see working in front of him.

These are not dishonest people. These are, in many cases, the most morally attentive people in the room.

And the argument they make is not wrong on its own terms. The money they redirect does reach real people. The good they do is visible and genuine. Compared to an abstract national treasury and its imperfect machinery, the direct transfer — rupee to human, cause to outcome — feels more honest, more efficient, more meaningful.

But the argument makes one assumption that does not survive scrutiny: that it is a choice between giving to the government and giving to good causes. It is not.

The tax is not optional. It is a prior obligation — the subscription fee for the functioning society inside which all acts of private generosity are possible. The doctor's free Saturday clinic exists in a city that has roads, electricity, and a functioning medical supply chain, all funded by the collective contribution of taxpayers. The cousin's siblings study in a country with universities, scholarships, and a legal system that protects the value of their degrees — all funded by the same pool. The NGO founder's cause reaches beneficiaries through a country with communications infrastructure, basic law and order, and a banking system — none of which private generosity built.

Private charity is not a substitute for civic contribution. It is a supplement to it. The two do not compete for the same rupee. They occupy different moral categories entirely.

There is also a harder truth inside this fortress. The "my money does more good" argument, however sincerely felt, assumes that the person making it has a better claim to decide how national resources are spent than the collective decision-making processes of a democracy — however imperfect those processes are. That is a significant claim. It is the claim of a person who has quietly appointed themselves as a one-person allocation committee for public funds. The generosity is real. The accountability is absent.

The truly generous person pays their full share to the system that makes their generosity possible — and then gives more on top of it. They do not treat one as an excuse to reduce the other.

Fortress Six does not hold.

4. THE THING NOBODY TOLD PREETHI — THE FORMAL ECONOMY IS HER GREATEST ALLY

The next morning, Ramesh finds Preethi making coffee in Arjun's kitchen before anyone else is awake. She is reading something on her phone, already in work mode at 7 AM on a Friday, the way people are when they genuinely love what they do.

Ramesh pours himself a cup and sits across from her. He doesn't intend to revisit last night's conversation. But something she said stays with him — specifically the phrase: "the system has taken enough from me already."

He thinks about it from her angle. Genuinely. And he realizes that there is something nobody has ever told Preethi — something that the tax conversation almost never addresses — and that it might actually matter to her more than it matters to him.

He says it carefully. Not as a lecture. As one equal to another, sharing information he thinks she might find useful.

"Can I show you something?" he asks. She looks up from her phone. He continues.

"You bought your apartment at 30. Alone. Your own loan, your own down payment, your own name on the title deed. That's extraordinary — I mean that genuinely. But do you know what made that possible? The bank approved your home loan because you had a clean, documented income trail. Your ITR for the last three years. Your Form 16. Your salary slips. Your financial identity — the paper version of your credibility — is entirely built on your declared, formal income."

Preethi is listening. Not defensively. She is the kind of person who listens when information is relevant.

"Now imagine you had been taking a significant portion of your income in cash for the last five years. Undeclared rental income, undeclared consulting fees, whatever it is. Your visible income would look smaller.

Your ITR would look weaker. The same bank might have offered you a smaller loan, or a higher interest rate, or asked for a larger guarantor. Your financial independence — the thing you worked the hardest to build — would have been quietly undermined by the very decision that felt like protecting it."

He pauses. Then adds:

"The formal economy is not the system that takes from you. It is the system that proves you exist — professionally, financially, legally. For a woman who has built everything herself, that proof is not a bureaucratic formality. It is armour."

Preethi is quiet for a moment. She sets down her phone.

Ramesh continues, gently. "There's more. If you ever want to start your own company — and I think you will, at some point — your ITR history is your founding document. Investors look at it. Banks look at it. Your credit history, your loan eligibility, your ability to scale — all of it traces back to how visible your income has been over time. Every rupee you kept invisible was a rupee that didn't build your financial identity. And your financial identity, for someone like you, is worth more than the tax you'd have paid."

He is not finished, but he stops himself. He has said enough. The rest is for her to think through.

Preethi nods slowly. She picks up her phone again. But Ramesh can see that she is not reading it anymore. She is thinking.

5. THE REALIZATION — FROM EXHAUSTION TO SOVEREIGNTY

What happens next does not happen in a single moment. It happens in the way most real decisions happen — gradually, then suddenly.

Over the next few weeks, Preethi finds herself returning to the conversation on the rooftop and the one in the kitchen. She is an engineer by training and a product manager by practice — she thinks in systems. And she begins to see the system she has been operating in with new clarity.

She has spent ten years building a career defined by transparency and meritocracy. She declared her talent openly and demanded to be paid for it fairly. She declared her ambition openly and refused to let it be diminished. She declared her independence openly and structured her entire financial life to protect it. In every dimension of her professional life, visibility has been her weapon and her shield.

And then, in this one dimension — the rental income, the twenty thousand rupees a month — she retreated into the shadows. Not because she is dishonest. Because she is tired. Because the system has asked so much of her, and in this one small space she wanted to feel like something was entirely hers, unaccounted for, unmonitored, free.

She understands this now for what it is. Not freedom. Exhaustion wearing the mask of freedom.

The formal economy did not create the exhaustion. The exhaustion was real and its causes are real — a system that has historically asked more of women while offering them less in return, that has under-represented them in the rooms where policies are made, that has not always been designed with their financial realities in mind. These are legitimate grievances. They deserve to be fought.

But the way to fight a system that has under-served you is not to **withdraw from it.** Withdrawal weakens you. It removes your financial footprint, your legal standing, your credit identity, and your moral authority to demand change. The way to fight a system that has under-served you is to become so **visibly, undeniably present within it** that it cannot ignore you. To pay your full share and then stand at the front of the room and say: I funded this. Now serve me accordingly.

Preethi has never backed down from any room in her professional life. She has no intention of starting now.

She opens her laptop. She logs into the income tax portal. She updates her rental income declaration for the year.

It takes eleven minutes.

She closes the laptop and makes another cup of coffee. She feels, unexpectedly, like herself.

6. THE TRANSITION — FROM THE ROOFTOP TO THE COUNTER

Back in Mumbai, a few days after his Bengaluru visit, Ramesh sits with the memory of both conversations — the rooftop and the kitchen — and feels something clarify inside him.

He has examined the six fortresses. He has watched an intelligent, principled woman dismantle her own most carefully constructed one. He has felt the pull of each argument personally and walked through why each one collapses under honest scrutiny.

And what he is left with is not a feeling of moral superiority. He does not feel like someone who has passed a test that others failed. He feels something quieter and more useful: clarity.

The stories we tell ourselves about why our individual contribution doesn't matter — they are not the conclusions of rational analysis. They are the conclusions of rational-sounding analysis performed in the service of emotional relief. They are the mind's way of making peace with a choice the heart has already made for reasons of exhaustion, resentment, or simple convenience.

They feel like arguments. They function as permissions.

And the antidote to a permission is not a counter-argument. It is a **decision.** A quiet, personal, renewable decision that you make not because the system has earned it — the system is imperfect and will always be imperfect — but because **you have.**

You have earned the right to stand in the sunlight of the formal economy. You have earned the right to say: I contributed my full weight. I know exactly what I paid for. And I have the standing to demand that it be spent well.

Ramesh picks up his keys. He needs to buy paint and electrical fittings for a small renovation he has been putting off. He knows a hardware store nearby — a man named Gupta Ji who has been a reliable supplier for years.

He has heard that Gupta Ji usually offers a "discount" for cash purchases. No bill, no GST, no record.

Ramesh walks to the store. He already knows what he is going to say.

The country you want is the country you pay for.

The stories we tell ourselves are the most powerful forces in our economic lives — more powerful than policy, more powerful than enforcement, more powerful than incentive. They determine what we declare and what we hide, what we contribute and what we withhold, what kind of nation we are building and what kind we are leaving behind.

When the story is "the system doesn't deserve my honesty," the nation gets the system it deserves.

When the story is "I am a sovereign who funds this republic and demands its full performance in return," the nation gets the citizens it needs.

Preethi changed her story in eleven minutes on a laptop in Bengaluru. **Ramesh has been living his for thirty years.** The difference was never intelligence or integrity. Both are present in abundance. The difference was information — about the system, about the consequences, about the true cost of the fortress walls we build to protect ourselves from a truth we already know.

Now you have the information too.

What story will you tell yourself from here?

— ❖ —

Chapter 8
The Shadow Economy

The Parallel Republic That Feeds on the Formal One

This is that moment — the one Ramesh had already decided his answer to before he walked in the door.

Ramesh is at a local hardware store to buy paint, electrical fittings, and high-grade copper wiring for his home renovation. The total comes to Rs. 45,000. The air in the shop is thick — a heavy, chemical scent of turpentine mixed with the metallic tang of galvanised steel. Above him, a sputtering ceiling fan cuts through the humid heat, its rhythmic clicking sounding like a countdown.

The shopkeeper, Gupta Ji, a man Ramesh has known for a decade, leans over the scratched glass counter. He looks at the calculator, then at Ramesh, his voice dropping to a conspiratorial, friendly register. "Sir, you are an old customer. Why waste money? If you want a proper GST bill, the price will be Rs. 53,100 because of the 18 percent bracket. But if you pay in cash, I will give it to you for Rs. 44,000. No bill, no record, no tension. Why give Rs. 9,100 to the government so they can waste it? Keep it for your family."

Ramesh pauses. His hand is already on his wallet. The Rs. 9,100 difference is not just a discount. It is a month's worth of fuel, a high-end educational tablet for his daughter, or a much-needed medical check-up for his mother. Gupta Ji frames it as a favour — a small act of rebellion against a distant, cold bureaucracy.

But in this moment, Ramesh is standing at a crossroads. He is being invited to join the Shadow Economy — a parallel universe that breathes our air, drives on our roads, and eats our food, but refuses to contribute to the skeleton of the nation. Gupta Ji is not just offering a discount. He is offering Ramesh a membership in a Parallel Republic that thrives by cannibalising the formal one.

1. THE SCALE OF THE MISSING GDP — THE GHOST NATION

To understand the Shadow Economy, we must look at the sheer, terrifying scale of what is hidden. This is not just a few shopkeepers avoiding taxes. It is an entire ghost nation living within our borders.

Economists and global bodies like the IMF and the World Bank estimate that India's informal or shadow economy ranges between 20 and 45 percent of the reported GDP. If we take a conservative estimate of 25 percent, the math is staggering. With India's GDP currently hovering around $3.7 Trillion, a 25 percent shadow economy means nearly $925 Billion worth of economic activity goes unrecorded every single year.

The Hidden India — By the Numbers	What That Money Could Have Built
~$925 Billion in unrecorded economic activity annually	Larger than the entire GDP of Saudi Arabia, Switzerland, or Turkey
Cash component in real estate inflates property prices by 30–40%	Home ownership permanently out of reach for the salaried Ramesh
Rs. 1.98 Lakh Crore in GST evasion detected by DGGI in 2023	Nearly 10% of total annual GST collection lost to fake invoicing alone
Significant portion of India's gold held as frozen Black Gold	Wealth that does not circulate, does not create jobs, does not compound

When this much money stays in the shadows, it becomes Anemic Capital. It exists in physical form — stacks of notes in cupboards or kilograms of gold in lockers — but it is dead to the nation. It cannot be taxed to build cancer hospitals. It cannot be officially invested in the stock market to drive the next tech unicorn. And it cannot be used by the banking system to lower interest rates for honest home-seekers.

2. THE MECHANICS OF EVASION — THE PARASITIC MACHINE

The Shadow Economy is not a disorganised mess. It is a sophisticated, multi-layered machine designed to bypass the national pulse. It operates through three primary channels — what we might call the Leach Lines of the formal economy.

Mechanism	How It Works	The Damage Done
Circular Trading & Fake Invoicing	Paper companies generate fake invoices to claim Input Tax Credits that were never paid	Rs. 1.98 Lakh Crore stolen from the treasury in 2023 alone via this single method
The Benami Cycle	Shadow cash parked in land bought in the names of drivers, cooks, or non-existent relatives	Artificial land scarcity — a young engineer on Rs. 15 Lakhs cannot afford a 2-BHK metro apartment
Black Gold	Excess cash converted into gold biscuits and jewellery — frozen, invisible to the taxman	Wealth locked out of the productive economy — no jobs created, no capital compounded

Each of these mechanisms does double damage. First, it steals revenue directly from the treasury. Second, it distorts the real economy — inflating land prices, freezing productive capital, and pushing ordinary citizens like Ramesh further from the life they are working toward.

3. THE SMART MAN'S FINANCIAL TRAP — THE COST OF BEING A PULLER

Gupta Ji thinks he is being smart. He thinks he has outrun the system. But the Shadow Economy has a built-in Self-Destruct Mechanism. Because Gupta Ji hides his income, his Paper Power is zero. On his Income Tax Returns, he shows a meagre profit of Rs. 4 Lakhs a year to stay below the tax bracket. Two years later, when he wants to expand his shop or send his son to a university in the UK, he goes to a bank. The bank looks at his papers and says: Sir, you are poor. We can only give you a loan of Rs. 5 Lakhs.

But Gupta Ji needs Rs. 50 Lakhs. He is forced to go to the unorganised sector — local moneylenders and Shroffs. They do not care about papers. They only care about his property as collateral. They charge him 2 to 3 percent interest per month.

What Gupta Ji Chose	What It Cost Him	What Honesty Would Have Given
Hid income — showed Rs. 4 Lakhs profit on paper	Bank offers only Rs. 5 Lakh loan	Formal ITR unlocks Rs. 50 Lakh business loan
Avoided 18% GST	Forced to borrow at 24–36% annual interest from moneylenders	Business loan available at 9–11% from a bank

Kept the shop small to stay under the tax radar	Dukan stays a Dukan — forever a small shop	Formal growth path: hire 50 people, build a Brand
Parked cash in gold and Benami land	Capital frozen — dead to the economy	Money in formal system compounds at 12–15% in mutual funds

By staying in the shadows, Gupta Ji has capped his own growth. His Dukan will always stay a Dukan. It will never become a Brand. He chose to stay small and afraid rather than large and transparent — and the shadow economy rewarded him with exactly that: permanent smallness.

4. THE SHADOW SURCHARGE ON RAMESH — THE FREELOADER TAX

This is the most bitter pill for the honest taxpayer to swallow. The Shadow Economy is not a victimless crime. It is a direct tax on honesty.

Governments have fixed expenses: defence, infrastructure, salaries for teachers and police, and debt servicing. If the government needs Rs. 20 Lakh Crore to run the country and 25 percent of the economy is hidden, that entire Rs. 20 Lakh Crore must be extracted from the remaining 75 percent.

If the missing 25 percent — the Gupta Jis and the cash-only contractors — came into the light, the tax burden on Ramesh would plummet. If the tax base were to double, the tax rate for Ramesh could potentially be cut from 30 percent to 15 percent without the government losing a single rupee of revenue.

Because Gupta Ji evades, Ramesh pays a Freeloader Surcharge. Every time Ramesh sees that TDS deduction on his payslip, he is effectively paying for the road that Gupta Ji's delivery trucks use for free, the electricity grid that powers Gupta Ji's shop, and the army that protects the borders so Gupta Ji can do business in peace.

The Lazy Group are not just staying behind. They are standing on Ramesh's shoulders. They are the anchors slowing down the ship while Ramesh is in the engine room, sweating to keep the propellers turning.

5. THE GLOBAL PERSPECTIVE — HIGH TRUST VS. LOW TRUST

Why do countries like Denmark, Singapore, or Norway function with such clinical efficiency? It is not just because they are small or wealthy. It is because they are High Trust Societies.

Indicator	High Trust Society (Denmark / Singapore)	Low Trust Society (Shadow Economy Default)
Shadow Economy Size	Below 5–7% of GDP	20–45% of GDP

Why People Pay	Direct ROI visible — pothole-free roads, world-class schools, real safety net	No visible ROI — so citizens justify not paying to "level the field"
The Cycle	Virtuous — more compliance funds better services, which earn more compliance	Vicious — Jugaad is celebrated, integrity is mocked, race to the bottom accelerates
Global Investor View	Transparent, predictable — capital flows in freely	Opaque, unpredictable — investors fear a game where rules change based on who pays cash

India, historically, has been a Low Trust Society. We assume the politician will steal, so we justify our own stealing. We assume the neighbour is cheating, so we cheat to level the playing field. This creates a Race to the Bottom. In a Low Trust Society, Jugaad — clever bypassing of rules — becomes a national hobby, and integrity is mocked as a weakness.

This cultural rot is more expensive than the lost revenue. It prevents us from becoming a global superpower because global investors and innovators fear a lack of transparency. They do not want to play a game where the rules change based on who is paying in cash.

6. THE TECHNOLOGICAL SUNLIGHT — THE SHRINKING SHADOWS

For decades, the shadows were deep and wide. But the sun is rising. Data is the new sunlight.

The government's Digital India push is not just about convenience. It is about Enforced Integrity. The linkage of PAN, Aadhaar, and GSTIN has created a Digital Web that is becoming impossible to escape. Project Insight — the Income Tax Department's AI and machine learning system — now scans for Mismatched Lifestyles. If Gupta Ji declares an income of Rs. 4 Lakhs but buys a Rs. 60 Lakh luxury SUV or takes three foreign vacations a year, the AI flags it instantly. When Ramesh pays via a QR code, a digital footprint is created that cannot be erased with a cloth. Even small vendors are now part of the formal data stream.

In the last decade, the number of people filing tax returns has jumped from roughly 3.8 crore to over 8 crore. This is not just a sudden surge in patriotism. It is the realisation that the cost of staying in the shadows is now higher than the cost of coming into the light. In modern India, if you are invisible to the taxman, you are also invisible to the bank, the visa office, and the property registrar.

7. THE LAZY GROUP AND THE STAGNATION OF POTENTIAL

We must address a second, equally dangerous group: those who choose to stay in the informal sector simply because it is easier. These are not aggressive evaders. They are individuals and businesses that refuse to upskill, refuse to digitise, and refuse to grow because growth brings scrutiny.

A formal business that grows hires 50 people, provides ESI and PF benefits, and creates a middle-class ecosystem around it. An informal business that stays small hires two people in cash, provides no safety net, and keeps those families in perpetual instability. The multiplier effects run in opposite directions — one builds, one stagnates.

Laziness in compliance is not a private choice. It is a National Opportunity Cost. We cannot become a ten trillion dollar economy by being a nation of small shops hiding in the dark. We need Engine Entities — large, transparent, and globally competitive.

8. A CHOICE OF LEGACY — THE BILL AS A BALLOT

As Ramesh stands at the hardware counter, looking at Gupta Ji's expectant face, he realises that this Rs. 9,100 is more than just money. It is a vote.

If he takes the cash discount, he is voting for Shadow India. He is voting for the potholes, the corrupt local official, the high interest rates, and the inflated property prices. He is voting for a country that stays Developing forever because its citizens are too clever to be honest.

If he demands the bill, he is voting for the ten trillion dollar India. He is saying: I am a shareholder in this Republic. I am putting my money in. And because I am paying my GST, I now have the moral authority to stand at the local ward office and demand that this road be fixed. I have the right to demand that my daughter's school be world-class.

The Bill is a Voter's Act. It is the transition from being a Subject who hides from the state to a Sovereign who funds the state.

"Gupta Ji," Ramesh says firmly, pulling out his card. "Give me the bill. I want the GST invoice. I'm renovating my house, and I want to make sure the foundation of my country is just as strong as the foundation of my home."

Gupta Ji looks surprised, perhaps even a little disappointed. But as he begins to type the invoice into his computer, the sputtering fan above seems to hum a bit more steadily. The shadows in the corner of the shop seem just a little bit thinner.

The Shadow Economy is a ghost that haunts India's potential. Every time a Ramesh demands a bill, a part of that ghost disappears. It is time we stopped feeding the ghost and started building the house.

— ❖ —

Chapter 9

How Non-Payers Hurt Every Citizen

The High Cost of the Free Ride

The morning air in Mumbai is a thick soup of humidity and diesel fumes. Ramesh is walking his eight-year-old daughter Priya to her school bus stop. The walk is a daily obstacle course. The pavement is a jagged patchwork of broken concrete and exposed wiring, forcing them to step off the curb and walk on the very edge of the asphalt.

Just as they navigate a particularly deep puddle, a white luxury SUV — a vehicle that costs more than Ramesh's apartment — roars past. It does not slow down for the standing water. A wall of muddy, grey sludge erupts from under its tyres, drenching Ramesh's trousers and splashing across Priya's white school socks.

Ramesh stands frozen, the cold mud seeping through his clothes. He knows the owner of that SUV. It belongs to Mr. Khanna — the same neighbour whose CA manages his books so perfectly that he shows a net loss every year, paying zero income tax despite his fleet of cars and international vacations.

As Ramesh wipes the mud off his clothes with a handkerchief, he realises a bitter truth that no government hoarding will tell him: the man in the SUV is a thief of public space. He is using the road, but he did not help pay for it. He is enjoying the security of the city's police force, but he is not contributing a rupee to their salaries. He is relying on the national grid for his air conditioning, but he is dodging the very system that builds the power plants. In the cold language of economics, Mr. Khanna is a Free Rider. He is travelling on Ramesh's ticket — and his free ride is the reason the pavement is broken in the first place.

1. THE MATHEMATICS OF THE INFRASTRUCTURE GAP — THE NATIONAL DEBT TRAP

To understand why the pavement is broken, we must look at the Funding Gap. Every year, the Union Budget is a high-stakes balancing act. The government sets a Tax Target based on the projected needs of 1.4 billion people. When a large section of the wealthy and the informal middle class avoids tax, the government faces a structural revenue shortfall.

When the money does not come in through the Sunlight Economy, the government is left with two catastrophic choices.

Choice	What the Government Does	Who Pays the Price
I	Starvation of Services — cut spending on Quality of Life: parks, pavements, school labs, public clinics	Ramesh. He walks on broken pavements, studies in under-equipped schools, waits in overcrowded hospitals

II	The Debt Spiral — borrow from global markets to fill the revenue hole left by non-payers	Priya. One in four rupees the government spends goes to interest payments — a Rs. 11 Lakh Crore annual bill handed to the next generation

Because Mr. Khanna wants a tax-free life today, Priya will have a debt-burdened life tomorrow.

2. THE QUALITY OF SERVICE — YOU GET WHAT YOU DON'T PAY FOR

The most common anthem of the Indian middle class is: "Why should I pay? The public services are terrible!" This is the ultimate Chicken and Egg fallacy. Ramesh agrees that the services are poor — but he understands the Correlation of Compliance.

Consider the Doctor-to-Patient Ratio. The WHO recommends 1 doctor per 1,000 people. India struggles at roughly 0.7 per 1,000. To bridge this gap, the state needs massive capital to build AIIMS-level hospitals and fund medical research.

When a wealthy businessman or high-earning professional evades tax, they are not just saving money. They are stealing a bed from a rural health centre. They are removing a ventilator from a government ICU. They are deleting a seat from a subsidised medical college. When the missing 25 percent of the economy stays in the shadows, the government is forced into a Priority Trap — it can only afford to keep people from starving; it cannot afford to make them thrive. The non-payer traps the entire nation in Survival Mode, preventing the transition to a developed, high-functioning society.

3. THE SOVEREIGN CREDIT PENALTY — WHY YOUR HOME LOAN IS EXPENSIVE

The damage of the non-payer extends far beyond India's borders. It hits our standing on the global stage. A country's strength is measured by its Sovereign Credit Rating. Rating agencies like Moody's, Fitch, and S&P look at a country's Tax-to-GDP ratio to decide its financial health.

Metric	India	OECD Average
Tax-to-GDP Ratio	**~11%**	**~34%**
Sovereign Credit Rating	A few notches above Junk status	Investment Grade — A or above
Home Loan Interest Rate	~9% — because the nation is seen as risky	3–4% — because compliance is high
Who Pays the Difference?	**Ramesh — in EMIs every single month**	Nobody — lower rates are the honesty dividend

Because the nation is seen as risky due to its low tax base, the government and Indian corporations have to pay a Risk Premium — higher interest rates — when they borrow money from global markets. This high cost of capital trickles down through the entire banking system directly into Ramesh's monthly EMI. Mr. Khanna's tax saving is the reason Ramesh's home loan is so expensive every single month.

4. THE INFLATIONARY PRESSURE OF BLACK MONEY — THE DEATH OF THE HOUSING DREAM

Non-payers and evaders do not keep their saved money in transparent bank accounts — that would leave a digital trail. Instead, they park this wealth in assets that can absorb large amounts of undocumented cash: real estate and gold.

This creates an artificial, toxic scarcity of land. Property prices in Indian metros have outpaced salary growth by a staggering margin. A 2-BHK apartment that should naturally cost Rs. 60 Lakhs based on construction costs and land value is priced at Rs. 1.5 Crore. Why? Because black money has turned real estate from a utility — a place to live — into a laundry machine — a place to hide cash.

Ramesh's struggle to own a home — the decades of EMIs and the tiny square footage — is a direct result of the non-payer's need to store hidden wealth. The evader is not just hurting the government. They are effectively pricing Ramesh's children out of the housing market before they are even old enough to work.

5. THE PUSHERS AND THE PULLERS — AN ECONOMY OF TWO

To understand the full weight that falls on Ramesh's shoulders, we must be clear about who is carrying the boat and who is riding in it.

	The Pushers — The 3%	**The Pullers — The Lazy Group**
Who they are	Ramesh, Akash — formal sector workers who pay taxes and drive GDP	Cash-only micro-businesses, informal professionals who refuse to upskill or comply
What they contribute	The engines of the ten trillion dollar dream — income tax, GST, formal employment	Consume public resources — fuel, roads, stability — while producing the bare minimum
Role in the national boat	The Rowers — hands blistered, backs breaking, providing all forward momentum	The Anchors — some sleeping, some complaining, some splashing water on the rowers
Net effect on Ramesh	None — Ramesh is already carrying his weight	**Every Puller adds weight to Ramesh's oar. Every hidden oar slows the whole boat.**

When a large segment of the population decides to be content with less to avoid the headache of tax and compliance, the nation loses its competitive edge. This collective laziness is a National Opportunity Cost. We cannot become a superpower if our primary cultural value is Jugaad — finding shortcuts — rather than Excellence — building systems.

6. THE EROSION OF THE SOCIAL CONTRACT — THE SOCIOLOGICAL HAEMORRHAGE

Beyond the numbers and the economics, there is a deeper, more invisible wound: the destruction of the Social Contract. A nation is not just a piece of land. It is an agreement — the belief that if we all contribute according to our capacity, we will all progress according to our potential.

When Ramesh sees Mr. Khanna thriving while dodging his share, that contract is violated. The rupture does not stop at resentment. It cascades into three distinct and dangerous sociological failures.

When the Contract Breaks	What Ramesh Sees	What It Costs the Nation
Rise of Cynicism	"Why should I be the only honest person? Is my integrity just stupidity?"	When honesty is mocked, the moral fibre of the nation thins — compliance collapses from the inside
Brain Drain	The most talented, honest professionals leave for countries where tax paid = quality of life received	We lose our best minds because we let the Pullers dominate the domestic narrative

Class Friction	The salaried class begins to deeply resent the business and informal classes	A nation divided by tax-resentment cannot stand united against global challenges

Each of these collapses feeds the next. Cynicism breeds brain drain. Brain drain deepens class friction. Class friction breeds more cynicism. It is a spiral that no government scheme can reverse — only a culture of honesty can.

7. THE BOAT METAPHOR — ROWERS AND PASSENGERS

Imagine the Republic of India as a massive wooden boat on a turbulent sea, heading toward the distant shore of a ten trillion dollar economy. There are 100 people in this boat.

Three people are the Rowers — the taxpayers. They are straining every muscle, their hands blistered and their backs breaking. They are the only ones providing forward momentum. Ramesh is one of them.

Ninety-seven people are the Passengers. Some are sleeping. Some are complaining about the heat. Some, like Mr. Khanna, are standing on the deck, splashing water on the rowers and demanding the boat move faster.

Every time a Passenger refuses to take up an oar to save their energy, the weight on Ramesh's muscles becomes heavier. Every time a Passenger hides an oar under their seat to avoid being asked to row, the boat slows down.

Look at the rowers' hands.

Not their faces — their faces are turned forward, eyes on the shore. Look at their hands. The palms are thick with callus built over years of the same motion: grip, pull, release, grip, pull, release. The skin at the base of each finger is hardened where the oar has pressed, month after month, year after year, April after April. In the places where the wood has worn through the toughened skin, there are blisters — small, honest wounds that no one sees and no one asks about.

Ramesh has rower's hands. So does Akash. So does Vikram, who files his returns on Sunday mornings when other men are sleeping. So does Priya, who will one day develop her own calluses on her own salary slip.

They have never complained about their hands. They do not consider their hands unusual. They assumed, for a long time, that everyone in the boat had hands like theirs.

Now look at the passengers. Their hands are soft. Not because they are weak people — many of them are capable, intelligent, and in other areas of their lives, hardworking. Their hands are soft because they have never held the oar. They have spent the journey with their hands in their laps, or wrapped around a cup of tea, or gesturing expressively as they explain to anyone who will listen exactly what the rowers are doing wrong.

Mr. Khanna's hands are the softest in the boat. He has opinions about the direction. He has opinions about the speed. He has detailed, confident opinions about the quality of the rowing. He has simply never rowed.

The rowers do not ask for sympathy. They ask for one thing only: that the passengers look at their own hands, pick up an oar, and understand that the shore is real, the distance is finite, and the boat moves faster when more people pull.

The Free Ride is a myth. The boat does not move by magic; it moves by labour. If the three rowers collapse from exhaustion, the boat does not just stop — it sinks. The Free Ride is an act of Economic Sabotage. When you have the capacity to row but choose to sit, you are not a passenger. You are an anchor.

8. THE SILENT VICTIM — THE FUTURE INDIA

The ultimate victim of the non-payer is not the current government. It is the Future Version of India.

Every Rupee Withheld by an Evader Is...	...A Future Stolen From Someone
A micro-chip that was never researched	India remains an importer of technology, not an exporter
A rural road that remains a dirt track	Millions of villages stay cut off from markets and opportunity
A teacher who was never hired for a village school	A generation of children educated below their potential
A cleaner river that remains a sewer	Public health crises that cost far more to fix than to prevent
A startup that never got seed funding because capital was frozen in a gold locker	The next Infosys or Flipkart that never existed

As Ramesh watches the luxury SUV disappear into the neon-lit distance of the city, he realises he is not just angry about the mud on his trousers. He is angry because that SUV is driving on a road he built, toward a future he is funding, while the owner of the SUV is just along for the ride.

The Free Ride is never free. Someone, somewhere, is paying the price in sweat, in EMIs, and in missed opportunities. Ramesh picks up his bag, takes his daughter's hand, and continues the walk. He is tired — but he refuses to stop rowing. Because he knows that if he stops, the dream of the ten trillion dollar India dies with him.

He is the backbone. He is the engine. And it is time the passengers realised that the free ride is over — it is time to pick up an oar.

— ❖ —

Chapter 10

When Contentment Becomes Complacency

The Invisible Ceiling and the Nation It Traps

It is 2041. Ramesh is sixty-one years old.

He sits in a government hospital waiting room in Mumbai, a folder of medical reports on his lap, his reading glasses perched at the edge of his nose. The room smells of phenyl and waiting. The chair is plastic and hard. Around him are a dozen other people — some older, some his age — all of them waiting for the same specialist who is running two hours behind schedule.

His daughter, Priya, sits beside him. She is thirty years old now. She is a data analyst at a mid-sized firm. She is good at her job, talented, and deeply honest — just like her father raised her to be. She has been trying for three years to buy a 2-BHK apartment in the city where she grew up. Last month, she was told the waiting list for a government housing scheme had 18,000 applicants ahead of her. The private market is simply out of reach — property prices in this city never corrected because decades of black money kept them artificially inflated.

Ramesh looks at Priya. He feels a familiar, quiet weight in his chest. Not guilt — he paid his taxes honestly for thirty-five years. Not regret — he worked hard, raised her right, and gave everything he had. The weight is something else. It is the slow, dawning realization that the country he faithfully funded did not grow fast enough, did not widen its tax base quickly enough, did not shake its culture of comfortable stagnation in time — and Priya is the one living in the result.

He thinks of all the Vinays he has known over the years. The brother-in-law who chose Netflix over upskilling at forty. The colleague who stayed cash-only for fifteen years to "avoid the headache." The neighbor who boasted about his informal income while Ramesh's TDS quietly funded hospitals that now can't keep up with demand. He wonders: if even half of those people had contributed their fair share — financially, professionally, ambitiously — would this waiting room be different? Would Priya's apartment search be different?

The answer, he knows, is yes. And that answer is the subject of this chapter.

1. THE CONSEQUENCE CHAPTER — WHAT STAGNATION ACTUALLY COSTS

By now, this book has introduced you to the idea of the "Puller" — the citizen who consumes national infrastructure without meaningfully contributing to it. In Chapter 2, we met Suresh, who settled for "Bas Chal Raha Hai" on a Sunday morning balcony. We understood his psychology, his comfort zone, his quiet retreat from ambition.

But Chapter 2 asked: Who is this person? Chapter 10 asks a harder, more urgent question: What happens to a nation when millions of this person exist simultaneously, decade after decade, without correction?

This is not a chapter about diagnosing the problem again. This is a chapter about the bill that arrives when the problem is left unpaid. Because in economics, as in life, every deferred cost arrives eventually — with interest.

The Vinays of India — the healthy, capable, educated citizens who chose the comfort zone over contribution — are not simply "missing" from the national ledger. They are a compound liability. Every year they stagnate, they fall further behind. Every year they avoid the tax net, the burden on honest taxpayers grows heavier. Every year they choose "just enough," the nation loses the productivity it needs to fund its own future. And unlike a missed EMI, this kind of debt does not come with a reminder notice. It accumulates silently, invisibly, until one day it appears — in an overcrowded hospital waiting room, in a daughter's unaffordable apartment search, in an economy that is growing but somehow never quite arriving.

2. THE DEMOGRAPHIC DIVIDEND EXPIRES — THE TICKING CLOCK NOBODY MENTIONS

India's greatest economic asset in the 21st century has been described, celebrated, and debated in every budget speech, every policy paper, and every investor presentation for the last two decades: the Demographic Dividend.

The logic is seductive in its simplicity. India has a median age of approximately 28. More than 65% of its population is between 15 and 64 — the working age bracket. This means India has an unusually large proportion of citizens who are potentially earning, spending, contributing, and building. If harnessed correctly, this demographic structure could propel India from a developing economy to a developed one within a single generation.

The operative phrase is: if harnessed correctly.

Because here is what the budget speeches and investor presentations tend to omit: the Demographic Dividend is not a permanent feature. It is a time-limited opportunity with a hard expiry date. Demographic projections suggest that by approximately 2040, India's working-age ratio will begin to decline as the population ages. The window within which a large, young, energetic, tax-paying workforce can build the infrastructure, savings, institutions, and social security systems needed to support an older India is roughly fifteen years wide.

Fifteen years. That is not a long time in the life of a civilization.

Now consider what the Vinays of India are doing with those fifteen years. They are spending them in the comfort zone. They are spending them in low-productivity, low-complexity roles that generate minimal tax. They are spending them in the informal cash economy, invisible to the treasury. They are spending them watching news debates about the government's failures while contributing nothing to the government's capacity to correct those failures.

Every year a capable, working-age Indian chooses stagnation over growth, they are not simply "staying still." They are **burning a non-renewable resource.** The demographic window does not pause for the comfortable. It closes on schedule, whether or not the nation was ready.

And when it closes — when India's dependency ratio rises, when more citizens are retired or aging than are actively earning and contributing — the question will not be "Why didn't Vinay upskill?" The question will be: "Who is going to pay for all of this?" The answer, already visible in embryonic form today, will be: Priya. Ramesh's daughter. The next generation of honest taxpayers, carrying a load they did not create, funding a future they inherited already mortgaged.

India's Current Median Age	**~28 Years** *Working-age population: 65%+ of total*

Estimated Demographic Window	**~15 Years** *Before dependency ratio begins rising (~2040)*

The comfortable citizen who tells himself he is simply "living in peace" is, in the coldest macroeconomic terms, spending his country's most valuable non-renewable asset on personal comfort. The Demographic Dividend is India's one great structural gift. The Vinays are unwrapping it slowly, using it for nothing, and leaving the empty box for Priya's generation.

3. THE AI RECKONING — COMPLACENCY MEETS ITS MOST DANGEROUS ENEMY

Vinay, Ramesh's brother-in-law, has worked in the same mid-sized logistics firm for twelve years. He knows the old systems better than anyone in the office. He is the person people go to when the legacy software throws an error that the IT team cannot decode. This is his professional identity and his professional security blanket.

He does not know it yet, but that blanket is on fire.

We are living through what economists and technologists are calling the Fourth Industrial Revolution — a structural transformation of the global economy driven by Artificial Intelligence, automation, and machine learning. Unlike previous industrial revolutions that primarily displaced physical labor, this one is targeting cognitive, routine, middle-complexity tasks. The very tasks that the "comfortable" Indian professional has spent a decade perfecting.

Logistics coordination. Data entry. Invoice processing. Compliance reporting. Inventory management. Route optimization. Customer service scripting. These are not hypothetical targets — they are already being automated, partially or fully, by AI systems that work faster, make fewer errors, and cost a fraction of a human salary.

The profile of the person most vulnerable to this wave is strikingly specific: a professional between 35 and 50, who has reached a comfortable level of expertise in a narrow domain, who has not significantly upskilled in the last five years, and who operates in a role of moderate complexity that feels indispensable but is actually highly replicable by pattern-recognition software. In short: Vinay. Multiplied by millions.

Now trace the consequence of this displacement through the national ledger.

When Vinay loses his job to automation — not because he did anything wrong, but because he stood still while the world moved — three things happen simultaneously. First, he stops paying income tax. His direct contribution to the national treasury, already modest due to years of low-ambition, goes to zero. Second, his consumption contracts sharply. He stops buying branded goods, stops eating at restaurants, stops spending on the premium GST brackets that fund national infrastructure. His indirect tax contribution collapses alongside his direct one. Third, he may eventually require state support — healthcare subsidies, job retraining programs, social welfare. He transitions from a neutral passenger in the national boat to an active drain on its resources.

The complacent citizen is not simply a **missed opportunity** today. He is a **future liability** tomorrow. And the honest taxpayer — the Ramesh, the Akash, the Priya — will be asked to fund both the present infrastructure and the future safety net for the person who chose comfort over contribution.

The AI reckoning is not coming for the ambitious. It is coming for the comfortable. The professional who upskilled, who took the night course, who mastered the new tool, who pushed through the discomfort of learning — that person is not being replaced by AI. That person is being empowered by it. The one who settled, who said "I know enough," who treated the Sunday evening as purely a time for rest rather than growth — that person is the one the algorithm is quietly learning to replace.

This is not a moral judgment. It is a mathematical one. And the math falls hardest not on the comfortable person alone, but on every honest taxpayer who will subsidize the fallout.

4. THE MIDDLE PLATEAU AND THE TAX CEILING — NUMBERS THAT DO NOT LIE

Let us be precise about what the comfortable stagnation of the Indian middle class actually costs the national treasury. This is not a philosophical argument. It is arithmetic.

India's Tax-to-GDP ratio currently hovers around 11%. The OECD average — the benchmark of nations India aspires to join — is approximately 34%. This gap is not primarily the result of the very poor failing to contribute. The very poor are largely exempt from income tax, and this is as it should be. The gap is primarily the result of the vast, capable, earning middle layer — the Vinays, the Gupta Jis, the informal professionals — choosing to contribute at far below their actual capacity.

Consider this: if India's Tax-to-GDP ratio were to rise from 11% to even 18% — still well below the OECD average — the additional annual revenue at current GDP levels would be in the range of several lakh crore rupees. Not borrowed. Not printed. Earned, by a wider, more honest, more ambitious contributing population.

What would that money build? It would build the AIIMS hospitals that currently have five-year waiting lists for specialist appointments. It would build the metro rail networks that would free millions of Rameshs from two-hour daily commutes that consume productive hours and generate nothing. It would fund the primary school teachers needed to bring India's student-to-teacher ratio to a level where a child in a government school receives genuine attention rather than crowd management. It would service national debt without cutting infrastructure budgets. It would, over two decades of compounding, transform India's Sovereign Credit Rating from its current position to something that would halve the interest rate on every home loan in the country.

All of this is arithmetically available. None of it is politically radical. It simply requires that the comfortable middle — the Vinays — step up to their potential. Not to sacrifice. Not to suffer. Simply to grow.

Every percentage point of GDP that stays in the informal, stagnant, non-contributing economy is a percentage point of hospital beds, school classrooms, and clean water pipelines that does not get built. The comfortable citizen's leisure is not privately funded. It is, in the most literal sense, funded by Ramesh's TDS deduction — month after month, year after year, for a lifetime.

5. THE SOCIAL STABILITY BOMB — WHEN THE COMFORTABLE MAJORITY TURNS RESENTFUL

There is a third consequence of mass complacency that is rarely discussed in economic circles because it lives not in spreadsheets but in psychology and political science. It is, however, the most dangerous of the three.

When a society stratifies into a small, ambitious, high-contributing layer at the top and a large, comfortable, low-contributing layer in the middle, something corrosive begins to happen over time. The comfortable layer, having chosen stagnation for years, eventually looks upward at the ambitious layer and does not see inspiration. It sees inequality. It sees unfairness. It sees people who "got lucky" or "had connections" or "benefited from a rigged system." It begins to vote for policies that punish success rather than policies that create the conditions for broader success.

This is not a hypothetical scenario from a political theory textbook. It is a pattern that has played out in economies across the developing world. When the productive minority carries the nation while the comfortable majority watches and stagnates, the political equilibrium eventually shifts. The majority, feeling left behind, demands redistribution rather than growth. Tax the rich. Cap the salaries. Punish the "fat cats." These are not the demands of the desperately poor — the genuinely poor tend to be pragmatic about growth. These are the demands of the comfortable middle, who chose comfort over ambition and then resented the gap that opened between themselves and those who did not.

The Ramesh of today, the honest taxpayer who funded the roads and the hospitals and the satellites — the person this entire book has been written to honor — could find himself, in twenty years, politically outnumbered by the Vinays. And the Vinays, having never paid their full share, could vote to take more from the Rameshs. This is not justice. It is the predictable outcome of a society that romanticized comfort and mocked ambition for too long.

Complacency is not merely an economic problem. It is a **democratic time bomb.** When the comfortable majority eventually becomes the resentful majority, the ambitious minority — the very people who kept the lights on — become the target.

The only antidote is a culture shift. A society that genuinely celebrates ambitious citizens as its heroes — not as "greedy" or "showing off" — creates the conditions in which the comfortable middle aspires upward rather than resenting upward. The taxpayer must be made visible, celebrated, and respected. And the comfortable citizen must be made to understand that their stagnation is not a private choice. It is a political act with consequences that will eventually circle back to them.

6. VINAY'S REAL COST — A LEDGER THE NATION NEVER SEES

Let us return to Vinay specifically, because he deserves a fair accounting. Vinay is not a bad man. He is generous with his family, kind to his neighbors, and deeply patriotic in the abstract sense — he will argue passionately about national pride at a dinner table. He is simply comfortable. He has drawn his ceiling low and called it the sky.

But what does Vinay's comfort actually cost the nation over the course of a career?

Assume Vinay works from age 25 to age 60 — thirty-five years. Assume that for the first ten years, his low income genuinely limits his contribution, and we hold him blameless for that period. But from age 35 onward — twenty-five years — Vinay has the capacity to earn more, upskill, move up the value chain, and contribute meaningfully. Instead, he plateaus.

In those twenty-five years, a Vinay who chose growth over comfort — who took the certification course, who pushed for the promotion, who moved from the informal to the formal economy — might reasonably have doubled his effective tax contribution. That additional contribution, compounded across twenty-five years, represents not just money but everything money becomes: hospital equipment, road maintenance, school teachers, scientific research, defense readiness.

Now multiply Vinay by ten million. Because there are not one Vinay in India. There are tens of millions — spread across every city, every industry, every income bracket above subsistence. The collective "comfort tax" they impose on the national treasury is not a rounding error. It is a structural deficit that shows up every year in underfunded public services, every budget cycle in difficult trade-offs between healthcare and infrastructure, and every decade in a growth rate that is impressive but never quite enough to make the transformational leap.

The nation never sends Vinay a bill. But the bill exists. And Ramesh pays it. And Priya inherits whatever Ramesh could not cover.

7. THE INTERGENERATIONAL THEFT — WHAT PRIYA'S GENERATION INHERITS

There is a word for the practice of spending today and leaving the debt for those who come after: intergenerational theft. We usually apply it to government borrowing — the idea that a government that borrows excessively is mortgaging the future of children who had no voice in the decision. This is a valid critique. But there is another form of intergenerational theft that is less visible, less discussed, and equally damaging.

It is the theft that occurs when an entire generation of capable, educated, healthy citizens chooses to contribute below their potential — leaving the infrastructure underfunded, the tax base narrow, the social services strained — and then hands that underdeveloped country to their children.

Priya did not choose to grow up in a country with a 11% Tax-to-GDP ratio. She did not vote for the informal economy. She did not benefit from the cash-only transactions that kept the treasury thin. She simply arrived — talented, honest, hardworking — into a world partly shaped by the choices of those who came before her. The comfortable ones. The stagnant ones. The "Bas Chal Raha Hai" ones.

She is paying for their peace.

Her home loan is more expensive because the nation's Sovereign Credit Rating is depressed by a narrow tax base.

Her hospital appointment takes longer because the public health system is underfunded relative to what an honest, fully-contributing citizenry could have built. Her career opportunities are partially constrained by infrastructure gaps — slower internet in some regions, unreliable power in others, transport networks that could have been built a decade earlier if the money had been there.

Every child born to an honest taxpaying family in India inherits two things from their parents: the values of integrity and hard work, and the **consequences of everyone else's comfort.** This is the deepest injustice of the complacency culture — it does not hurt the comfortable. It hurts their children.

8. WHAT A NATION OF PUSHERS WOULD LOOK LIKE — THE OTHER FUTURE

It is worth pausing, before the final section of this chapter, to imagine the alternative. Not as a fantasy, but as a genuine possibility — because it is one. The numbers support it. The demographics permit it. The only missing ingredient is a collective cultural decision to choose it.

Imagine that over the next fifteen years — within the Demographic Dividend window — India's comfortable middle makes a different choice. Not all of them. Not overnight. But meaningfully, directionally, in sufficient numbers to shift the aggregate.

Imagine that a significant portion of the informal sector gradually formalizes — not because of enforcement alone, but because the cost-benefit calculus shifts as digital infrastructure makes compliance easier and the benefits of formal status (credit access, social security, professional legitimacy) become more visible and valuable.

Imagine that the culture of "Chalta Hai" begins to be replaced — in schools, in families, in media — by a culture that genuinely celebrates the ambitious taxpayer as the nation's hero. Not the billionaire who escaped to Dubai. Not the politician cutting a ribbon. The Ramesh. The Akash. The honest professional who pushed themselves, paid their share, and demanded accountability in return.

What does that country look like?

It looks like a Tax-to-GDP ratio that climbs from 11% to 18% within a decade — without a single rate increase. Just a wider base. Just more people contributing their honest share.

It looks like public hospitals with the equipment and staffing they need, because the treasury has the resources to fund them properly.

It looks like Priya finding an affordable apartment, because black money is no longer artificially inflating property markets to hide evaded income.

It looks like a Sovereign Credit Rating that attracts foreign investment at lower cost, which creates jobs, which generates more taxpayers, which funds more infrastructure, which attracts more investment. The virtuous cycle that every economist knows is possible but that requires the cultural foundation of a contributing, ambitious citizenry to initiate.

This is not utopia. It is arithmetic. It is what happens when the Vinays of India decide — individually, personally, without waiting for the government to force them — that their potential is a national resource and not a personal luxury.

9. PRIYA'S QUESTION — THE CHAPTER'S FINAL MIRROR

Back in the hospital waiting room, Priya looks up from her phone and studies her father's face. She has known that expression since childhood — the quiet, inward look he gets when he is thinking about things larger than the room he is sitting in.

"Papa," she says softly, "are you okay?"

Ramesh looks at her. He smiles — the real smile, not the reassuring one. "I'm fine," he says. "Just thinking."

She waits. She has always been good at waiting for him to finish his thoughts.

"You know," he says finally, "I paid my taxes for thirty-five years. Every month, without fail, before the money even reached my account. I paid for the roads. I paid for the defense. I paid for the hospitals." He pauses and looks around the waiting room. "I just wish more people had paid alongside me. It would have been a different wait."

Priya is quiet for a moment. Then she asks the question that has been sitting at the back of her mind for years — the one she never quite found the right moment to ask.

"Do you think they knew? The ones who didn't pay — do you think they understood what they were doing to people like us?"

Ramesh considers this for a long time.

"No," he says at last. "I don't think they did. I think they thought it was private. Their choice, their money, their life. I think they thought the country was big enough and strong enough to absorb their absence." He folds his hands on the folder of reports. "They didn't understand that the country is not a machine that runs by itself. It runs on people. On the ones who show up. Who contribute. Who push even when pushing is hard."

Priya nods slowly. She opens her laptop. She has a tax filing to complete — for her own returns, which she has been preparing with meticulous honesty. She has never, in her working life, hidden a rupee of income. She learned this from her father, the same way she learned to ride a bicycle and to read and to believe that doing the right thing matters even when it costs you.

She types quietly for a few minutes. Then she looks up again.

"I'm going to pay," she says. Not about the tax form in front of her. About something larger. "Whatever it takes. However hard it gets. I'm going to contribute my full weight. Because someone has to."

Ramesh puts his hand over hers. The waiting room is still full. The specialist is still late. The country is still a work in progress.

But somewhere in that exchange — between a father who gave everything and a daughter who intends to do the same — the only answer that actually matters is spoken.

The country does not belong to those who consume it. It belongs to those who build it. And building it means paying for it — honestly, fully, and without waiting for someone else to go first.

Ambition is not greed. It is citizenship.

The comfortable citizen who settles for less is not harming himself alone. He is narrowing the tax base that funds the hospitals, roads, and schools that his own children will need. He is consuming the Demographic Dividend without contributing to the infrastructure it was supposed to build. He is voting, with every year of stagnation, for a smaller, slower, more indebted India.

The ambitious citizen — the one who pushes, who upskills, who earns more and pays more and demands more — is not just building a better life for themselves. They are building the floor beneath every other citizen's feet. They are the load-bearing columns of the Republic. They are, in the most literal and unromantic sense, the reason the country functions at all.

The $10 Trillion India is not a government project. It is not an election promise. It is a sum. It is the aggregate total of individual decisions made by hundreds of millions of people — to grow or to stagnate, to contribute or to consume, to push or to pull. Every person who chooses growth adds to that sum. Every person who chooses comfort subtracts from it.

Ramesh paid his share. **Priya will pay hers.** The question this chapter leaves with you is simple, direct, and personal: **Will you pay yours?**

— ❖ —

Chapter 11

The Honest Man's Burden

When the System Fails the People Who Feed It

1. THE MAN WHO TRIED TO DO EVERYTHING RIGHT

There is a South Mumbai cafe that Ramesh and Vikram have been meeting at since their twenties. It is the kind of place that has not changed its menu in fifteen years — filter coffee in steel tumblers, idli that arrives without being asked, a ceiling fan that wobbles at a specific speed that neither too fast nor too slow. It is a place that feels, in a city of relentless reinvention, like a small act of resistance against time.

Vikram is already there when Ramesh arrives. He is sitting at their usual corner table, a stack of printed documents beside his chai, reading something on his phone with the focused frown of a man who has been reading too many documents for too long. He looks, Ramesh thinks as he sits down, about ten years older than he should.

Vikram is forty-one. He runs a mid-sized logistics technology company — fifteen employees, two offices, one in Pune and one in Hyderabad, clients across four states. He started it at thirty-two, nine years ago, with savings he had built over a decade of corporate employment and a conviction that India's supply chain needed smarter software. By any reasonable measure, he has succeeded. His revenues are growing. His clients renew. His team is competent and loyal.

He is also, as he explains over the next forty minutes, exhausted in a way that has nothing to do with the work itself.

"I'll tell you what my last Sunday looked like," he says, setting down his phone. "I woke up at seven. I had three GST reconciliation notices to respond to — my vendors filed late, which creates mismatches in my returns that I have to explain even though the fault is not mine. I spent two hours on that. Then I had a show-cause notice from the tax department about a TDS discrepancy from three years ago. Twelve thousand rupees. My CA says it's a data entry error on the portal's side. We have proof. But responding formally, with the right documentation, in the right format, before the deadline — that took another hour and a half." He pauses. "Then I made lunch for my kids."

Ramesh says nothing. He is listening.

"Here is what I don't understand," Vikram continues. "I went fully formal from day one. GST registered before I was even legally required to be. I pay advance tax. I file quarterly returns. I have never — not once — taken a cash payment or made an undeclared expense. I chose honesty as a business strategy because I believed it would pay off over time. And in many ways it has. My credit line is good. My clients trust me. I have a paper trail that proves I exist and what I have built."

He picks up the stack of documents. "But this is what honesty costs me every month. Twelve to fifteen hours of compliance work that produces nothing. No product. No service. No customer value. Twelve to fifteen hours of unpaid, unacknowledged labour I perform for the government every month in exchange for the privilege of being in the formal economy."

"And the man down the road who runs an identical business in cash — who employs the same number of people, serves the same clients, and earns roughly the same revenue — he spends zero hours on this. Zero. He uses that time to grow his business, spend time with his family, or simply sleep. And somehow I am the one the system is designed for?"

Meanwhile, across the city, Rajan is having a different kind of Sunday.

He runs an identical packaging supply business — fifteen employees, similar clients, comparable revenue. He has never filed a GST return. He has never responded to a show-cause notice, because none have ever arrived. His books show a modest income of Rs. 3.8 lakhs a year. His actual income is somewhere north of Rs. 40 lakhs. The difference lives in cash, in a drawer, in gold his wife keeps in a locker whose contents have never been declared to anyone.

This Sunday, Rajan woke up at eight. He had chai on the balcony. He watched his daughter's cricket match at the colony ground — she bowled out two batters and he cheered so loudly the other parents smiled. He had lunch with his family. In the afternoon he took a nap. By four o'clock he was at his brother-in-law's place for cards.

He did not think about GST reconciliation. He did not think about show-cause notices. He did not think about TDS discrepancies from three years ago. He thought about nothing that Vikram thought about.

He also drove to the cricket match on a road Vikram helped pay for. His daughter's school is funded by a budget Vikram contributed to. The police that keep his cash drawer safe are salaried by a treasury Vikram fills. He has never once considered this. Why would he? Nobody has ever asked him to.

He does not sound angry. He sounds tired. Which is somehow worse.

Ramesh holds his steel tumbler of coffee and thinks about this for a long moment. He knows Vikram well enough to know that this is not a complaint of someone looking for permission to quit. Vikram is not going anywhere. He will file the response to the show-cause notice. He will reconcile the GST mismatches. He will continue to be the honest man the system claims to want.

But Ramesh also knows that Vikram is not wrong. And that the full argument this book has been making — that honest citizens are the backbone of the Republic, that non-contributors drag the economy down — requires one more layer of honesty before it can be complete.

The honest man's burden is real. And it is time to name it.

2. THE GHOST IN THE MACHINE — INDIA'S COLONIAL TAX DNA

To understand why tax compliance in India carries the weight it does — why the Vikrams of this country feel not just burdened but vaguely betrayed — you have to go back further than the Income Tax Act of 1961. You have to go back to the psychological inheritance that Act itself was built upon.

For almost two hundred years, the Indian subcontinent was taxed by a foreign occupier. The British colonial revenue system was not designed to fund services for the people being taxed. It was designed to extract resources from them — to finance the East India Company's operations, to fund wars fought for British strategic interests, to send money home to London. The tax collector was not a public servant. He was an instrument of extraction. And the citizen who hid money from the tax collector was not an evader. He was, in the moral logic of the time, a patriot.

This is not a romanticization of tax evasion. It is a historical fact with a very long shadow. The psychological pattern that was drilled into multiple generations of Indians — that the tax collector is your adversary, that the government's claim on your income is fundamentally illegitimate, that cleverness in avoiding official financial scrutiny is a form of self-preservation rather than dishonesty — did not vanish on August 15, 1947.

It was transmitted. Parent to child, culture to culture, generation to generation, in the ten thousand small ways that values travel without being formally taught. The shopkeeper who keeps two sets of books learned it from his father, who learned it from his father, who learned it in an era when the only sensible response to the revenue officer's arrival was to hide what you had.

The flag changed in 1947. **The department's attitude, in many places, did not.** For the first three decades of independent India, the tax system operated in what economists now call the "Inspector Raj" mode — a culture of presumed guilt, discretionary harassment, and bureaucratic friction that felt, to many ordinary citizens, disturbingly similar to what had come before. You were not a citizen contributing to a shared national project. You were a subject being assessed by an authority that viewed your income with suspicion and your explanations with default disbelief.

This is the ghost that haunts Vikram's Sunday mornings. Not the GST portal or the show-cause notice in isolation — but the accumulated cultural weight of a system that has not yet fully made the transition from extraction to partnership. The new Income Tax Act of 2025 is the most serious attempt in six decades to exorcise that ghost. But ghosts do not disappear with legislation alone. They disappear when experience consistently contradicts the memory.

For now, the memory is still louder than the experience.

3. EIGHT HUNDRED SECTIONS — THE WOUND THAT BECAME THE SYSTEM

When the Income Tax Act was passed in 1961, it was built for a different India. The economy was simpler, largely agrarian, with a narrow base of formal income earners. The law reflected that simplicity — a workable if imperfect framework for a country in the early stages of building its tax infrastructure.

Then India grew. And every time it grew in a new direction — new financial instruments, new business structures, new digital transactions, new cross-border flows — the law responded not by redesigning itself but by adding. A new section here. A proviso there. An explanation inserted into an existing clause to clarify what the clause had failed to anticipate. Amendment after amendment, Finance Act after Finance Act, for sixty-four consecutive years.

The result, by 2024, was a statute of more than 819 sections spread across 47 chapters. Sections numbered not sequentially but alphabetically — 80C, 80CCC, 80CCD, 80CCD(1), 80CCD(1B), 80CCD(2), 80CCE, 80CCF, 80CCG — a numbering system that functioned as institutional memory for tax professionals and as an impenetrable wall for everyone else. Definitions were scattered across chapters, requiring readers to jump backward and forward through the statute to understand a single obligation. Exceptions were buried in sub-provisos to sub-clauses of sub-sections. The only people who could navigate it fluently were the people you paid to navigate it for you.

Income Tax Act 1961	**Income Tax Act 2025**
Total sections	**819+ sections reduced to 536**
Total chapters	**47 chapters reduced to 23**

Section numbering	**Alphabet-heavy (80C, 80CCD(1B)) replaced with sequential numbers**
Key concept	**'Previous Year' + 'Assessment Year' replaced by single 'Tax Year'**
Language	**Legal labyrinth replaced with plain, operational English**
Effective date	**Repealed from April 1, 2026**

For the Vikrams of India — the honest, formal-sector entrepreneurs who chose compliance — this complexity was not just inconvenient. It was a tax on their honesty. Every hour spent decoding the law, every rupee paid to a CA to explain what should have been self-evident, every Sunday morning consumed by reconciliation was a cost that their cash-only competitors did not bear. The complexity did not affect the shadow economy. It only burdened the people who were already trying to do the right thing.

This is the first and most fundamental failure of the old system: **it made honesty expensive.** And when honesty is more expensive than evasion, a rational person will at minimum be tempted by evasion, and a less-than-perfectly-principled person will choose it.

4. FIVE WAYS THE SYSTEM FAILED ITS MOST LOYAL CITIZENS

The complexity of the old law was not the only failure. There were five distinct structural problems — each one a legitimate reason why a reasonable, intelligent, otherwise honest person might find their commitment to compliance eroding over time.

Failure One — The Perception of a Broken Social Contract

Ramesh has a specific memory that he returns to when this argument arises. It is from three years ago. His father was scheduled for a specialist consultation at the government hospital nearest to their home — a consultation that required a referral, which required a separate appointment, which had a waiting time of six weeks. The specialist, when they finally saw him, spent eleven minutes with them.

Ramesh does not begrudge the specialist his eleven minutes. He understands that the doctor is seeing sixty patients a day in a system that is funded at a fraction of what it needs to be. But sitting in that waiting room — his father's medical file on his lap, his TDS column fresh in his memory from the previous month's salary slip — he felt the specific vertigo of a contract that had not been honoured.

He had paid. The service had not been delivered at the level the payment implied. Not because no one was trying — the nurses were working, the doctor was working, the administrative staff were working. But because the aggregate contribution of the nation was not sufficient to fund the system at the level the nation's health actually required.

This is the perception of a broken social contract. And it is not a perception born of ingratitude or ignorance. **It is the perception of a rational person who understands the basic exchange and can see, clearly, that one side is not keeping pace.** The response — whether conscious or not — is often to pull back. If the government is not delivering its end, why should I deliver mine?

The answer, as this book has argued, is that pulling back makes the delivery worse, not better. But the feeling that generates the question is real and deserves to be named as such.

Failure Two — The Asymmetry of Penalty

Vikram shows Ramesh a piece of paper. It is a notice from the Income Tax department about a TDS discrepancy of ₹12,000 from a payment made three years ago. The discrepancy has arisen because the vendor to whom the payment was made had a PAN mismatch in their own filings — a problem entirely outside Vikram's control.

The notice requires a formal written response with supporting documentation, filed within fifteen days, failing which penalty proceedings will be initiated. Vikram has already engaged his CA at a cost of ₹8,000 to prepare the response. He will likely spend ₹8,000 to defend against a ₹12,000 discrepancy that was not his fault.

Meanwhile, a large corporate house in the same industry carried a disputed tax demand of ₹340 crore for nine years through appeals, stays, and counter-appeals before a final resolution was reached. The cost of the nine-year delay — interest foregone on ₹340 crore — ran into tens of crores. The corporate had the legal resources to sustain the battle. Vikram, for ₹12,000, does not even have the option to contest without it costing more than the amount at issue.

This is the asymmetry of penalty. **The system is technically equal in law but profoundly unequal in practice.** The large entity can litigate indefinitely. The small honest entrepreneur absorbs the cost of compliance error — even when the error is not theirs — because the alternative is worse. This asymmetry is not just unfair. It is a direct disincentive to formalisation for every small business owner who watches it and concludes that the formal economy is a risk the informal economy does not carry.

Failure Three — The Absence of Visible Taxpayer Benefits

Ramesh thinks about a specific scenario sometimes. He has been employed continuously for twenty-two years. He has paid income tax on his salary every single month of those twenty-two years without a single default. He has contributed to the national treasury a sum that, compounded conservatively, represents a significant portion of what he has earned.

Now imagine that tomorrow his company announces a restructuring and his position is eliminated. He is fifty years old. He has two months of notice. He has savings — because he has always been careful — but those savings are finite. He begins looking for a new position.

What does the state provide for him in this moment of vulnerability? The state that has received his contribution every month for twenty-two years without exception?

In most OECD countries, the answer would include: unemployment insurance — a percentage of his last drawn salary paid for a defined period while he searches. Subsidized retraining programs if his skills need updating. Active employment exchange services. In some countries, a contributory pension that has been building on his behalf throughout his working life.

In India, the answer is: essentially nothing specific to his taxpaying history. The general safety net exists — subsidized ration, public health, basic infrastructure. But there is no mechanism that says: because you contributed honestly for twenty-two years, here is your proportional return in this moment of need. The contract is entirely one-directional in its visibility.

This is not an argument for not paying tax. It is an argument for why the system must **make the return on honest contribution more visible** if it wants to sustain and expand the culture of honest contribution. Invisible benefits breed visible resentment.

Failure Four — The Indirect Tax Burden Nobody Calculates

Consider a middle-class family's monthly budget — a family like Ramesh's. They pay income tax directly through TDS. But they also pay tax on almost everything they consume, often without realizing it.

Their mobile bill carries GST. The fuel for the family scooter carries both central excise and state VAT, with the effective tax rate on petrol exceeding 50% of the pump price. The health insurance premium carries 18% GST. The restaurant meal carries 5% GST. The packaged food items carry rates between 5% and 18% depending on category. The new television carries 18% GST. The air conditioner carries 28% GST.

When you add the direct and indirect tax burden of a typical middle-class Indian household, the effective tax rate as a proportion of gross income is significantly higher than the income tax rate alone suggests. A family with a reported income tax burden of 15% may have an effective total tax burden — direct plus indirect — of 25% to 30% of gross income. This is not a low-tax country for the honest formal sector citizen. It is a high-tax country with a narrow direct tax base, which means the indirect tax burden falls heavily on everyone regardless of whether they contribute directly.

The honest taxpayer pays twice: once through the income tax they declare, and once through the consumption taxes they cannot avoid. The shadow economy citizen pays only the consumption tax. **This double burden on the formal sector is the mathematical proof of what happens when the tax base is too narrow.**

Failure Five — The Complexity Cost Borne Only by the Honest

We return to Vikram's Sunday. Twelve to fifteen hours a month. Forty-eight thousand rupees a year in CA fees. Three years of records maintained at personal cost to respond to a three-year-old discrepancy. The compliance infrastructure that an honest small business must maintain is, itself, a significant operating cost that does not appear in any official measure of the tax burden.

The old Income Tax Act's 819 sections, its alphabet-soup numbering, its chains of provisos — these did not burden the cash economy operator. They burdened the formal economy operator exclusively. The complexity was not neutral. It was a tax on honesty, paid only by those who were already paying.

5. APRIL 1, 2026 — THE DAY THE SYSTEM FINALLY LISTENED

On August 21, 2025, the President of India gave assent to the Income Tax Act 2025. On April 1, 2026 — the first day of the new tax year — six decades of accumulated legislative scar tissue were formally set aside. The Income Tax Act of 1961 was repealed.

What replaced it is not perfect. Nothing that emerges from a parliamentary process ever is. But it is, by every honest measure, a significant and overdue act of institutional listening.

From 819 sections across 47 chapters, the new Act comes down to **536 sections across 23 chapters.** The reduction was achieved not by weakening enforcement or removing obligations, but by doing what should have been done years ago: consolidating related provisions, eliminating redundant language, and rewriting the remaining text in direct, operational English that a non-specialist can read without a law degree.

The infamous alphabet-heavy section numbering — 80C, 80CCC, 80CCD(1), 80CCD(1B) — is gone. In its place, simple sequential numbering across the entire statute.

The distinction between "Previous Year" and "Assessment Year" that confused taxpayers and generated disputes for decades is gone. In its place, a single unified "Tax Year" concept that aligns with how human beings actually think about time.

The new Act introduces mandatory notices before enforcement actions — a structural protection for the taxpayer that did not exist with this clarity before. It extends faceless, digital-first administration to speed up assessments and refunds while reducing the in-person interface that was historically a source of both harassment and corruption. It allows TDS refund claims even after missing the ITR deadline without penalty — a recognition that procedural failure should not permanently cost a citizen who was otherwise honest.

The ₹12 lakh basic exemption limit — meaning that individuals earning up to ₹12 lakh annually effectively pay zero income tax after rebates — remains intact, protecting the lower middle class from direct tax burden while the nation works to widen the base from the top down.

This Act is not the completion of a journey. It is a direction signal. It says, for the first time in a very long time, that the system is beginning to treat the taxpayer not as a suspect to be interrogated but as a **partner to be served.** That is not a small thing. In a country where the colonial ghost has haunted the revenue department for eight decades, it is, in fact, a very large thing.

Vikram reads about the new Act on his phone one evening after his children are asleep. He reads about the reduced sections, the plain language, the sequential numbering, the Tax Year concept. He reads about the faceless assessments and the mandatory notices.

He puts his phone down. He does not celebrate. He is too experienced for celebration — he knows that legislation and implementation are different things, and that the culture of an institution changes more slowly than the words in its statute book.

But something shifts. Not from burden to ease — not yet. From isolation to acknowledgment.

The system saw us. Finally. It did not thank us. But it acknowledged that what it was asking of us was too much. And in the language of institutions, that is what apology looks like.

6. TWO CATEGORIES — THE CRITICAL DISTINCTION

This chapter has spent considerable time making a case for systemic failure. That case is honest and necessary. But it must be paired with an equally honest and equally necessary distinction — because not everyone who avoids tax is Vikram.

There are two fundamentally different categories of non-contribution in India, and conflating them is both intellectually dishonest and strategically counterproductive.

Category One — The Systemic Victim

This is Vikram. This is the small entrepreneur who found the compliance cost of the old Act genuinely prohibitive. This is the first-generation professional in a small town who had no access to a CA, no knowledge of the filing portal, and no margin for error in a system that penalised mistakes asymmetrically. This is the daily wage earner whose income is irregular and whose understanding of tax law is limited by education and access. This is the self-employed consultant who received no Form 16, found the ITR form designed for salaried employees, and quietly gave up.

These people did not choose the shadow economy as a moral position. They arrived there through a combination of complexity, cost, inaccessibility, and institutional discouragement. The system failed them before they had a chance to fail the system. They deserve empathy, accessible pathways back to compliance, and the structural reforms that the new Act begins to provide.

Category Two — The Systemic Exploiter

This is not Vikram. This is the Khanna who earns forty lakhs a year from multiple income sources, employs a sophisticated CA firm, fully understands every provision of every Act, and uses that understanding not to comply but to structure deliberate non-compliance. This is the Gupta Ji who has operated cash-only for fifteen years not because the portal confused him but because the savings significantly exceed the risk, and the risk has always felt manageable.

These people are not victims of the system's complexity. They are exploiters of it. They use the system's genuine failures — its complexity, its asymmetric enforcement, its cultural tolerance of informal transactions — as convenient cover for choices that are fundamentally about self-interest rather than principled resistance. When the new Act simplifies the system, these people will not suddenly discover compliance. They will find new structures to avoid it. They require enforcement, not empathy.

The book's central argument — that non-contributors drag the economy down — applies **fully and without qualification** to Category Two. It applies **with significant qualification** to Category One, where the primary response must be systemic improvement rather than moral condemnation.

This distinction matters because it determines the right response. Category Two requires stronger enforcement, digital trail tracking, and cultural naming of deliberate evasion for what it is. Category One requires exactly what the new Act provides — simpler processes, accessible language, lower compliance costs, and an institutional attitude that treats the taxpayer as a partner rather than a suspect.

7. The Honest Man's Choice — Why Vikram Stays

Ramesh and Vikram have been at their corner table for over two hours. The filter coffee has been refilled twice. The lunch rush has come and gone around them.

"Do you ever think about going informal?" Ramesh asks. Not as an accusation. As a genuine question between two men who have known each other long enough for genuine questions.

Vikram is quiet for a moment. He picks up the stack of documents and taps them on the table edge to align them. It is the gesture of a man who is honest with himself before he is honest with anyone else.

"Yes," he says. "Every time I file a response to a notice that shouldn't exist. Every time I spend a Sunday reconciling someone else's error. Yes."

Ramesh nods.

"But here is the thing," Vikram continues. "If I go informal — if I take that step — I lose more than the compliance cost I save. I lose my credit line. I lose my large corporate clients who require formal invoices and GST compliance from their vendors. I lose the legal standing to sue if a client defaults. I lose, over time, the paper trail that tells the story of what I built. And I lose something else."

He pauses. Ramesh waits.

"I lose the standing to be angry. The informal operator cannot sit across from a politician at an industry forum and say: the system is failing honest businesses. Because the politician will look at you and say: are you a formal business? And if the answer is no — even partially no — the argument dies. The moral authority to demand a better system belongs exclusively to the people who are funding it."

He taps the document stack again. "These papers are not just my compliance burden. They are my credentials. They are proof that I showed up. That I paid. That I have the right to stand in this room and say: **I funded this Republic. Now serve me accordingly.**"

Ramesh thinks about this on the walk back to the station. He thinks about it on the train home, standing in the general compartment, one hand on the overhead rail, watching the city pass outside the window.

The honest man's burden is real. The colonial ghost is real. The asymmetric penalty is real. The broken social contract is real. The complexity cost is real.

None of it dissolves the obligation. What it does is transform its meaning.

You do not contribute to a perfect system. You contribute to a **repairable one.** And the act of contribution is itself the credential that gives you the authority to demand the repair. The Vikrams who stay formal — who absorb the burden, file the responses, pay the CA fees, maintain the paper trail — are not just building their own businesses. They are building the moral foundation from which reform can be demanded and sustained.

The system has begun to listen. The new Act is evidence. The faceless assessments, the sequential numbering, the Tax Year concept, the simplified language — none of it happened by accident. It happened because enough honest, formal-sector citizens — enough Vikrams — stayed in the system long enough to make their voices impossible to ignore.

The reward for staying was not immediate. It rarely is. But it came.

Stay in the sunlight. The system is learning to deserve you.

— ❖ —

Chapter 12

The Two-Way Contract

What the System Owes You — and What You Owe It Back

1. TUESDAY EVENING — A DIFFERENT KIND OF FILING

It is a Tuesday evening in April 2026. Vikram is at his desk in the Pune office, the city settling into its post-work quiet outside the window. His screen shows the new income tax filing portal. His accountant had sent him the pre-filled return that afternoon — already populated with his salary data, his TDS amounts, his bank interest, his GST-registered business income, all of it pulled automatically from the Annual Information Statement that the department had compiled from its own data sources.

He reads through it. He finds the sections using the new sequential numbering — not the old 80CCD(1B) alphabet maze that used to require a cheat sheet pinned above his desk, but clean numbers in a logical order that actually tells him where to look. He finds the Tax Year column — one unified concept replacing the old Previous Year and Assessment Year distinction that had confused him for nine years and his CA for approximately as long.

He makes three manual corrections — two investment declarations and one additional income entry. He uploads the supporting documents. He reviews the summary. He submits.

The acknowledgment appears on screen at 7:43 PM.

He sits back. He looks at the acknowledgment number. He feels something he has not felt after a tax filing in nine years of formal business operation. Not relief — he has always felt relief. Something different. Something that takes him a moment to name.

Normalcy. The filing felt like a normal administrative task performed by a normal adult citizen. Not a Sunday-morning ordeal. Not a CA-mediated translation of a language designed to exclude him. Not a compliance burden that cost him half a working day and a four-figure fee. A Tuesday evening task, done and dusted before dinner.

He calls Ramesh. They have been speaking about this for years — about what the system owes the people who fund it, about whether reform was possible, about whether the honest man's patience would ever be rewarded. Vikram does not make a speech. He simply says:

"Tuesday evening, Ramesh. It took a Tuesday evening. It used to take a Sunday."

There is a pause on the line. Ramesh understands exactly what that sentence means. He has filed his own return under the new Act that morning. He felt it too.

The system is changing. Not completely. Not perfectly. But genuinely. And this chapter is about what that change means, what still needs to happen, and — most critically — what the honest citizen owes in return.

2. GIVING CREDIT WHERE IT IS DUE — WHAT HAS ALREADY IMPROVED

Before arguing for what reform must still deliver, this chapter will do something that is both honest and strategically necessary: it will acknowledge what has already been delivered. Because the honest taxpayer who has waited for the system to improve — who stayed formal through the Inspector Raj era, through the 819-section labyrinth, through the paper-return years — deserves to know that their patience produced results.

The Income Tax Act 2025, effective April 1, 2026, reduced the statute from over 819 sections across 47 chapters to 536 sections across 23 chapters. It replaced alphabet-soup section numbering with sequential numbers. It replaced the confusing Previous Year and Assessment Year distinction with a single Tax Year. It rewrote the surviving text in plain operational English. This is the most significant structural reform of India's direct tax law since 1961. It happened because enough formal-sector citizens stayed in the system long enough to make the argument for simplification impossible to ignore.

Faceless Assessment — the system by which tax assessments are now conducted digitally and anonymously, without the taxpayer needing to appear before a specific officer — removed the in-person interface that was historically the primary point of harassment and corruption in the assessment process. It is imperfect in implementation but structurally sound in design. It treats the taxpayer as a file to be assessed rather than a person to be pressured.

The Annual Information Statement — the AIS — now aggregates a taxpayer's financial data from multiple sources: salary, dividends, bank interest, property transactions, securities trades, GST-registered business income. Pre-filled returns built on AIS data mean that most of a salaried taxpayer's return is completed before they open the portal. The information gap between what the taxpayer knows and what the department knows has narrowed dramatically.

UPI's 131 billion annual transactions have created a digital financial trail that makes large-scale informal cash transactions increasingly visible by contrast. The merchant who accepts only cash in a neighbourhood of UPI users is increasingly conspicuous. The digital economy is, slowly but structurally, making the shadow economy harder to sustain invisibly.

The ₹12 lakh effective zero-tax threshold — meaning individuals earning up to ₹12 lakh annually pay zero income tax after rebates — protects the aspirational lower middle class from direct tax burden while the nation works to widen the base from the top and from within the informal sector. This is sound policy: build the culture of formal participation before imposing the cost of formal taxation at the margin.

The honest assessment is this: **the Indian tax system has reformed more meaningfully in the last five years than in the preceding thirty.** That is not cheerleading. It is an honest accounting — the same kind the book has been asking of its readers throughout. The patient, formal, honest taxpayer is beginning to see the returns on their patience. The system has not arrived. But it has turned. And direction matters as much as destination.

3. THE UNFINISHED BUSINESS — THREE REFORMS THAT CANNOT WAIT

The simplification is done. The digital infrastructure is building. The acknowledgment has begun. But three critical structural failures remain — failures that, if left unaddressed, will limit the impact of everything that has already been achieved.

Reform One — The Taxpayer Loyalty Dividend

Vikram has been formally registered and fully compliant for nine years. His compliance history is clean. He has never once been the originating source of a genuine discrepancy. Every notice he has received has traced back to vendor errors, portal issues, or data mismatches outside his control. Yet today he receives exactly the same level of default scrutiny as a business that registered yesterday under pressure from a GST inspection team.

This is behaviorally irrational. Every loyalty program — airline frequent flyer miles, credit card reward points, long-tenure employee benefits — is built on the same fundamental insight: rewarding consistent behavior increases the probability of that behavior continuing. The tax system is one of the very few compliance frameworks in the world that provides zero marginal benefit for long-term loyalty. You pay for thirty years and receive the same default suspicion as someone who filed for the first time last month.

The reform is specific and implementable: a tiered compliance track system based on consecutive clean filing history. Taxpayers with three or more consecutive years of clean filings receive expedited assessments with a guaranteed 30-day completion window. Those with five or more years receive a lower audit probability threshold — their returns are flagged for scrutiny only when anomalies exceed a defined percentage variance from their own historical pattern, not against a population average. Those with ten or more years receive automatic fast-track refund processing with a seven-day credit guarantee.

This is not preferential treatment. It is rational resource allocation. The department's enforcement capacity is finite. Concentrating scrutiny on new filers, irregular filers, and pattern-anomaly filers — while giving clean long-term taxpayers a lighter-touch experience — serves both efficiency and fairness simultaneously.

Reform Two — The Annual Tax Impact Statement

Every year, within 30 days of the acknowledgment of a filed return, every taxpayer should receive a personalised Tax Impact Statement. Not a notice. Not a summary of their filing. A statement of what their specific contribution funded.

If Ramesh paid ₹1,80,000 in income tax in the previous Tax Year, the statement tells him: your contribution funded approximately 2.3 kilometres of national highway maintenance, 840 mid-day school meals, 0.4 square metres of government hospital infrastructure, and 1.2 hours of a government scientist's salary at ISRO. The numbers are approximate. The calculation methodology is public. The data is real.

This is not a marketing exercise. It is the most basic accountability mechanism a democratic government owes its primary funders. It makes the invisible visible. It closes the ROI question — the "what do I actually get for this?" question that every honest taxpayer has felt at least once — not with a philosophical argument but with a specific, personal, verifiable answer.

It also creates a feedback loop that no policy speech can replicate. When a taxpayer receives a statement showing that their contribution funded school meals, they become personally invested in whether those meals actually happen. They become, in the most literal sense, a shareholder demanding accountability from their investee. This is the civic transformation your book has been arguing for from Chapter 1 — and the Tax Impact Statement is the mechanism that makes it concrete, annual, and personal.

Reform Three — The Asymmetric Penalty Fix

Vikram spent ₹8,000 defending against a ₹12,000 notice that arose from his vendor's PAN mismatch — a discrepancy the department's own data systems could have identified as vendor-sourced rather than recipient-sourced within seconds of the query being run. This is not a rare edge case. It is a systematic pattern that affects hundreds of thousands of small formal-sector businesses every filing cycle.

The fix is structurally simple: for disputes below a defined threshold — say ₹50,000 — where the source of the discrepancy is demonstrably in the vendor's or counterparty's data rather than the taxpayer's, the system resolves automatically in the taxpayer's favour without requiring a formal response. The department already has the data to identify vendor-sourced discrepancies. The reform is the policy decision to use that data to protect the taxpayer rather than burden them.

For disputes above the threshold, a dedicated small taxpayer dispute resolution track — guaranteed response within 21 days, zero cost to the taxpayer, staffed by officers trained in service rather than assessment — replaces the current system where the taxpayer's only option is the same formal appeals process available to a corporate with a ₹340 crore dispute. The playing field is never going to be perfectly equal. But it should at least be navigable without a corporate-size legal budget.

4. THE TAXPAYER PRIVILEGE FRAMEWORK — WHAT LOYAL CITIZENS HAVE EARNED AND NEVER RECEIVED

Here is the argument that this book has been building toward since Chapter 1, and that no chapter has stated as directly as this one will.

In India today, paying your taxes honestly gives you exactly one thing: the legal right to not be prosecuted for not paying them. That is not a reward. That is the absence of a punishment. Meanwhile, the citizen who does not pay — who operates in cash, who earns informally, who contributes nothing to the national treasury — receives subsidized ration, subsidized LPG, free government healthcare, PM Awas Yojana housing, free grain under

PMGKAY, and the infrastructure built by other people's money.

The incentive structure of the Indian state is, in its current form, **behaviorally inverted.** The rewards flow toward non-contribution. The burdens flow toward contribution. And then the system wonders why the tax base is narrow.

Ramesh sits with this thought one evening, his salary slip on the table beside him. He is not angry — he has moved past anger into something more analytical. He is thinking about what a different incentive structure would look like. What it would feel like to be rewarded — genuinely, tangibly, visibly — for thirty years of honest contribution.

He imagines it specifically. Scene by scene. Benefit by benefit. And for the first time in thirty years of tax filing, the imagination does not feel bitter. It feels like a blueprint.

This is the Taxpayer Privilege Framework. Four tiers of recognition, reward, and respect that the honest contributing citizen has earned and that the Republic owes them in return.

Tier 1 — The Access Privileges — Your Time Is Valuable

Priority Government Service Lanes

At passport offices, RTO counters, government hospitals, railway reservation centers, and municipal corporation offices — a dedicated fast-track counter for taxpayers with a clean ITR filing history of three or more consecutive years. Not a different service. The same service, faster.

The way frequent flyers get priority boarding — not a better plane, but recognition of loyalty. Ramesh imagines showing his taxpayer identity at the passport office counter and walking past the two-hour queue to a ten-minute window. This is not privilege. This is proportional recognition of contribution.

Taxpayer Health Priority

Honest taxpayers with five or more consecutive years of ITR filing receive priority OPD registration at government hospitals and AIIMS — not a separate ward, not better doctors, simply a dedicated registration desk and a shorter wait. The person who funded the hospital is recognized at the hospital door. The symbolism alone — the moment when the government acknowledges, in a physical queue, that this person contributed — would be worth more to the honest taxpayer than the time saved.

Dedicated Taxpayer Service Channel

A taxpayer-specific grievance portal where responses are guaranteed within 48 hours, staffed by officers trained in service rather than assessment. Today, the department that sends you a notice also handles your complaint about the notice. The conflict of interest is structural. A dedicated service channel — staffed by people whose performance metric is resolution speed and taxpayer satisfaction rather than revenue recovery — breaks that conflict and treats the honest citizen as a customer, not a subject.

Tier 2 — The Financial Privileges — Your Honesty Should Pay

The Taxpayer Credit Score

A government-issued financial credibility score — separate from the CIBIL credit score — reflecting a citizen's taxpaying history. A clean five-year consecutive ITR filing history earns a high Taxpayer Credit Score. This score is shared with banks and NBFCs as a formal input in the loan approval process. The direct result: lower interest rates on home loans, personal loans, and business loans for taxpayers with strong compliance histories. Priya, filing her returns honestly from her first year of employment, would be building not just a tax record but a financial identity that reduces her borrowing cost for the apartment she is trying to afford. Her father's lesson is, literally, paying dividends.

Concessional Rates on Government Services

Train tickets on Rajdhani and Shatabdi at a 10% concessional rate for individuals with three or more consecutive years of ITR filing. Government museum entry, national park entry, and government-run tourism packages at taxpayer-concessional rates. The state subsidizes many things for many citizens — ration, fuel, fertilizer, healthcare. It should subsidize something specifically and visibly for the citizens who fund all those subsidies. This concession is not financially significant. Its significance is entirely symbolic: the state is saying, for the first time, that honest taxpaying has a reward that the taxpayer can feel in daily life.

Priority Allocation in Government Schemes

When a government housing scheme, a skill development program, or a business loan scheme is oversubscribed —

as almost all of them always are — taxpaying status with a clean filing history is a positive tiebreaker in the allocation process. The citizen who has contributed to the fund that finances the scheme has a legitimate claim to priority access within it. This is not charity. It is the most basic expression of the shareholder principle: those who invest in the enterprise have a first claim on its returns.

GST Input Credit Protection for Compliant Small Businesses

Vikram's specific pain — vendor-initiated GST mismatches creating ITC denial for the compliant recipient — is addressed through a dedicated small taxpayer ITC protection mechanism. A formal small business with a clean compliance history of three or more years is not penalised for upstream vendor failures they cannot control. The department's own data identifies the source of the mismatch. The protection is simply the policy decision to use that data in the taxpayer's favour.

Tier 3 — The Recognition Privileges — Your Identity Deserves to Be Seen

The Taxpayer Identity Card

A government-issued physical and digital card — not unlike Aadhaar but specifically for taxpayers with a minimum three-year consecutive filing history — that serves as proof of taxpaying status. It is scanned at the priority service counter. It is presented at the concessional rate window. It is a visible, pocketable identity document that says: I am a contributing citizen of the Indian Republic. Ramesh imagines pulling this card from his wallet with the same quiet pride he felt the day he received his first salary slip. Identity drives behavior. When honest taxpaying becomes something you carry and show, the culture around it changes — slowly, then all at once.

The Annual Taxpayer Acknowledgment Letter

Every year, within 30 days of a filed return, every taxpayer receives a personalised letter from the Income Tax Department. Not a notice. Not an acknowledgment number. A letter — addressed to them by name, stating the total amount they contributed in the previous Tax Year, stating in approximate proportional terms what that contribution funded, and signed by a senior official. This is what every honest taxpayer has deserved for their entire working life and never received. It is the thank you that the acknowledgment number never was. It is the moment when the invisible hero is finally, formally seen.

The Rajaswa Ratna — Public Recognition of Long-Term Taxpayers

A national register — publicly accessible and opt-in — of citizens who have filed ITR consecutively for 10, 20, or 25 years. A Rajaswa Ratna recognition — a taxpayer equivalent of the Padma awards — conferred annually on individuals who have contributed honestly over a long career, nominated by their peers and verified by the department. India celebrates its cricketers, its film stars, and its entrepreneurs with enormous institutional energy. It has no formal mechanism to celebrate the honest salaried professional who funded all the infrastructure those celebrated individuals grew up using. The Rajaswa Ratna corrects that silence. It says: building the nation with your taxes, year after year, without recognition, is an act of civic heroism. And heroes deserve to be named.

Tier 4 — The Institutional Privileges — Your Rights Deserve Protection

The Taxpayer Ombudsman with Real Power

A dedicated Taxpayer Ombudsman — independent of the Income Tax Department, reporting directly to Parliament — with the authority to order refunds, waive penalties, and direct assessments to be closed where evidence clearly supports the taxpayer's position. Today the taxpayer's only formal recourse is appeals within the same institutional hierarchy that issued the original notice. An independent Ombudsman changes the power dynamic structurally — creating an authority whose mandate is specifically the protection of the taxpayer's rights rather than the recovery of the department's revenue.

The Presumption of Honesty

For taxpayers with five or more consecutive years of clean filing history, all assessments begin from a presumption of honesty. The burden of proof in disputes shifts: the department must demonstrate error rather than the taxpayer demonstrate compliance. This is how it works in most OECD tax systems. It is how it should work here. The loyal, long-term, clean-record taxpayer should not be treated as a default suspect every time they file. They should be treated as what they are: a proven partner of the Republic, entitled to the benefit of the doubt they have spent years earning.

5. The Citizen's Reform — The Half of the Contract That Is Yours

Every reform proposed in this chapter is a reform the government owes the honest taxpayer. The Taxpayer Privilege Framework, the Three Remaining Reforms, the Annual Tax Impact Statement — these are debts the system has accumulated over decades of taking contribution without returning recognition.

But this chapter will not end there. Because this book has never been only about what the government owes. It has always been equally about what the citizen owes. And the two-way contract in this chapter's title requires both sides to be stated with equal clarity.

The citizen's reform is not a single policy change. It is a set of individual decisions — made privately, renewed annually, lived daily — by each person who has read this book and recognized themselves in its characters. Here is what each of those decisions looks like.

The Suresh Reform — Choose Ambition

Suresh, watering his balcony plants in comfortable stagnation, is not a villain. He is a man who has drawn his ceiling low and called it the sky. The Suresh reform is the decision to push that ceiling upward — not for abstract national reasons, but for the concrete reason that a growing citizen adds weight to the tax base and a stagnating one does not. Every rupee of additional income earned in the formal economy by a Suresh who chose to grow is a rupee that widens the base, reduces the burden on Ramesh, and funds the hospital that Suresh himself will use when he is sixty-five.

The Preethi Reform — Return to Full Visibility

Preethi, who declared everything from her salary and nothing from her rental income, is not a bad person. She is an exhausted person who drew a private line and called it pragmatism. The Preethi reform is the decision to erase that line — to recognize that the formal economy is not the adversary but the infrastructure, and that every rupee kept invisible quietly erodes the financial identity that full visibility would have built. She made her choice in eleven minutes on a Tuesday evening. Anyone who recognizes themselves in her story can make the same choice in the same amount of time.

The Gupta Ji Reform — Choose the Invoice

Gupta Ji, at his hardware store counter, offering a cash discount for a no-GST transaction, is not a criminal. He is a businessman managing margin in a system that made compliance expensive for too long. The Gupta Ji reform is the decision to choose the invoice anyway — to understand that the GST he collects is not his money being taken, but the public's money passing through him, and that his role in that passage is not extraction but contribution. The new Act has made compliance cheaper. The excuse of cost has weakened. The decision now is simpler than it has ever been.

The Vinay Reform — Spend the Demographic Window

Vinay, spending his Sunday evenings in comfortable contentment, is not wasting his own time. He is spending India's most valuable non-renewable resource — the demographic window that closes around 2040 — on personal peace. The Vinay reform is the decision to spend at least a portion of that window on growth, on upskilling, on earning more, on contributing more, on building the infrastructure that his own older self will depend on. Comfort is a destination. It should not be a starting point.

The Vikram Reform — Stay in the Sunlight

Vikram, sitting with his stack of compliance documents at the South Mumbai cafe, exhausted and questioning, is the most important reform case of all. Because Vikram is already doing everything right — and the temptation to stop is entirely understandable. The Vikram reform is the decision to stay. To file the response. To pay the CA fee. To maintain the paper trail. Not because the system deserves it yet — it doesn't, fully — but because the standing to demand that it improve belongs only to the people who are still inside it, still paying, still visible, still present.

The two-way contract cannot be demanded from only one direction. You cannot ask the government to deliver a Taxpayer Privilege Framework while simultaneously withholding the contribution that would fund it. You cannot demand the Annual Acknowledgment Letter while declaring only the income you cannot hide. You cannot ask for the Presumption of Honesty while operating a portion of your business on a presumption of invisibility. **The contract is mutual or it is nothing.**

6. Saturday Morning — Priya's First Filing

It is a Saturday morning in April 2026. Ramesh is sitting at the kitchen table with his laptop open and a cup of chai going cold beside it. Priya is across from him, her own laptop open, her first income tax return under the new Act on her screen.

She is twenty-five years old. She joined her company eight months ago. This is her first full Tax Year as a salaried professional — the first time she is filing as an earning, contributing citizen of the Indian Republic rather than as a dependent or a student.

She has been working on the return for forty minutes. She finds it manageable — the pre-filled data is mostly accurate, the sequential section numbers make logical sense, the Tax Year concept matches how she already thinks about the financial year. She has one question about a deduction for her professional development course, which Ramesh answers in two minutes.

At 10:47 AM she submits.

She looks at the acknowledgment number on her screen. She looks at her father.

"Is this it?" she asks. "Is this all it takes?"

Ramesh smiles. He thinks about his first filing — the paper forms, the physical submission, the 298-section-turned-819-section Act, the CA who charged him ₹2,000 to translate a document that should have been in plain language to begin with. He thinks about Vikram's Sunday mornings. He thinks about every year in between.

"Now," he says. "It takes this now. It used to take a Sunday."

Priya nods. She closes her laptop. She picks up her chai.

"Do you think it'll keep getting better?" she asks.

Ramesh thinks about the new Act. About Vikram's Tuesday evening. About the Taxpayer Identity Card that does not yet exist but should. About the Annual Acknowledgment Letter that has never been sent but must be. About the priority counter at the passport office and the concessional train ticket and the Rajaswa Ratna and the Ombudsman with real power and the Presumption of Honesty for the citizen who has earned it.

He thinks about the distance between what is and what should be. And then he thinks about the distance between where the system was and where it is now — the Tuesday evening, the sequential numbers, the Tax Year, the pre-filled return, the faceless assessment.

It has moved. It is moving. Imperfectly, slowly, incompletely — but genuinely.

"Yes," he says. "If we keep showing up. Yes."

Priya nods again. She opens her laptop to a different screen — she has work to finish before lunch. She is already thinking about the next thing. She is her father's daughter in the best possible way: she does what needs to be done and then moves forward.

Ramesh watches her for a moment. Then he closes his own laptop. He picks up his cold chai. He thinks about the two-way contract — what the system owes, what the citizen owes back, the long and imperfect negotiation between them that has been running since 1947 and that his daughter has just, without fanfare, joined.

The country you want is built by the citizen you choose to be.

Every reform in this chapter requires the government to act. Every reform also requires the citizen to show up — formally, honestly, fully, and without waiting for perfection before beginning. The system is imperfect and improving. The citizen's obligation does not wait for the improvement to be complete. It precedes it. It enables it. It is, in the most fundamental sense, the only thing that makes the improvement possible.

Pay your share. Demand your recognition. Hold the system to its half of the contract. And never, for a single Tax Year, let the system's imperfection become your permission to step back from yours.

— ❖ —

Chapter 13

The Shareholder Life

How the Identity Changes Everything

1. The Morning After — Sunday, April 2026

It is the Sunday after the Saturday morning when Priya filed her first return.

Ramesh woke at the usual time. Made chai. Read the paper. Did nothing remarkable. And yet something in the texture of the morning is different — not dramatically, not in any way he could easily explain to someone who asked. Simply different. Quieter. More settled.

He thinks about Priya at the kitchen table yesterday, laptop open, asking: is this it? Is this all it takes? He thinks about his own answer: now, yes. It used to take a Sunday.

He thinks about what she did not know she was doing in those forty minutes. She was not just filing a return. She was opening an account. Not with a bank — with the Republic. She was making the first deposit in a ledger that will define her financial identity, her legal standing, her credit history, and her moral authority as a citizen for the next four decades. She was, without knowing it, doing the most consequential administrative act of her adult life.

And she did it on a Saturday morning, with one question, before lunch.

Ramesh finishes his chai. He gets dressed. He has somewhere to be.

There is a ward-level public meeting today — a monthly grievance session at the local municipal office, the kind Ramesh has walked past for years without going in. He has always had a reason not to: too busy, too pointless, too frustrating. The decisions are made before anyone arrives. Nobody listens. What is the point?

This morning, for the first time in thirty years of paying taxes, he does not have that reason. He goes in.

2. The ITR as Financial Passport — What Priya Built in 40 Minutes

Before we follow Ramesh into that meeting, let us be specific about what Priya actually created on Saturday morning. Because the honest taxpayer almost never understands the full value of what they are building, year by year, in the act of filing.

Priya is twenty-five. She has one year of formal employment, one filed ITR, and a modest salary. By the conventional metrics of financial identity — credit score, assets, collateral — she is at the beginning. But she has already done the most important thing.

She has made herself visible.

In three years, when she applies for a home loan, the bank will not be assessing just her current salary. It will be assessing her financial story — the three consecutive years of declared income, the clean ITR history, the evidence of formal employment and formal contribution. That story is worth more than any single number on her payslip. It is the difference between the bank offering her their best rate and their cautious rate. Over a twenty-year home loan, that difference is not marginal. It is lakhs.

White Money Has Velocity

Consider the alternative — the shadow-economy version of Priya. Same salary, same city, same ambitions. But she takes a portion of income in cash, declares the minimum, keeps the rest invisible. Her paper income looks smaller. Her ITR looks thinner. When she applies for the loan, the bank looks at the document and sees a woman of limited means, not the woman of real means she actually is.

The cash felt like freedom. The ITR told a smaller story. And a smaller story is worth less at every counter she will ever stand at.

Gupta Ji has stacks of cash in a locker. That cash is a prisoner. It cannot be deposited without triggering a notice. It cannot be invested in equities or mutual funds without creating a paper trail that contradicts his declared income. It cannot be used as proof of funds for a visa application. It cannot be shown to a bank as collateral for a business loan at reasonable rates. **Shadow money exists. It does not live.**

Ramesh's money is in the formal system. It has been working for him for thirty years — in the loan that got him his apartment at a rate Gupta Ji could not access, in the SIP that has been compounding quietly since his late twenties, in the credit line that allowed him to handle his father's medical emergency without borrowing from a moneylender at 24 percent interest.

The Compounding Edge

Over twenty years, formal money invested in equity mutual funds at a market average return significantly outperforms informal cash sitting in gold or under a mattress losing value to inflation. This is not a speculation. It is the arithmetic of the formal economy — the economy that Priya just formally joined on Saturday morning.

Her forty-minute filing was not paperwork. It was the opening chapter of a financial biography that will compound in her favour for the rest of her working life. Every year she adds to it honestly, the document becomes more valuable — not just to the government, but to her.

The honest taxpayer does not just fund the nation. **The honest taxpayer funds themselves.**

3. The Virtuous Cycle — One Number That Changes Everything

There is a single number that connects Ramesh's monthly TDS deduction to Priya's future home loan EMI. It is India Tax-to-GDP ratio.

Today that number sits at approximately 11 percent. The OECD average — the benchmark of the nations India aspires to join — is approximately 34 percent. That gap is not primarily the result of the very poor failing to contribute. The very poor are largely exempt, and rightly so. The gap is the result of the vast capable-and-earning middle layer — the Vinays, the Gupta Jis, the Preethi-before-the-kitchen-conversation — choosing to contribute at far below their actual capacity.

Now trace what happens when that number moves. Not to 34 percent. Just to 18 percent. Still well below the OECD average. Still a realistic, achievable target within a decade if the cultural shift this book is arguing for takes hold in sufficient numbers.

The Chain Reaction

At 18 percent Tax-to-GDP, government revenue increases by several lakh crore rupees annually without a single rate increase. Just more people contributing their honest share. With that additional revenue, the government borrows less from domestic capital markets to fund its deficit. When the government borrows less, it stops competing with private citizens and businesses for the available pool of money. When that competition reduces, the cost of borrowing falls. Interest rates come down — not by government decree, but by the logic of supply and demand in the money market.

When interest rates fall, Priya's home loan is cheaper. Not by a symbolic fraction. By percentage points that, over twenty years, translate into lakhs of rupees she keeps rather than pays to the bank.

Every Vinay who chooses to grow rather than stagnate, every Gupta Ji who issues the invoice, every Preethi who logs into the portal and declares the rental income — each one is a fractional contribution to a chain reaction that ends in **Priya's home loan being cheaper.** The connection is invisible. The mathematics is not.

The comfortable citizen who says my small contribution does not matter has not done this calculation. Their stagnation is not a private choice. It is a vote against

Priya's future. And it costs her money she has not yet earned.

4. The Voice That Cannot Be Taken Away

The municipal meeting is already in session when Ramesh arrives. It is held in a ground-floor room of the ward office that smells of dust and old files. A ceiling fan rotates slowly overhead. Twelve people are seated in plastic chairs facing a table at which two officials sit with the slightly glazed expression of people who have been nodding at complaints for an hour.

Ramesh takes a seat at the back. He listens.

The complaints are familiar. The drain on the east side of the lane has been blocked for three months. The streetlight at the crossing has been out since October. The footpath outside the new building has not been repaired after the construction damage. Each complaint is received with a nod, a notation in a register, and a vague assurance about forwarding the matter to the relevant department.

Nothing will happen. Everyone in the room knows nothing will happen. The assurances are the ritual conclusion of a ritual complaint. The register exists to absorb grievances, not resolve them.

Then a younger man — perhaps thirty, software professional by the look of him — leans forward and says: I filed an RTI last month about the footpath repair budget for this ward. The allocated amount was released in November. It is now April. I would like to know where that money went.

The room shifts. The officials exchange a brief look. The nodding slows.

Ramesh watches this and feels something recognise itself in him.

The young man is not angry. He is not dramatic. He has simply done the one thing that changes the entire dynamic of the exchange: he has come with evidence of contribution and a specific, documented question that cannot be absorbed by a nod and a register entry.

The RTI Is Not a Weapon. It Is a Receipt.

The Right to Information Act gives every citizen the right to ask any government body for information about its activities. But in practice it is used overwhelmingly by journalists, activists, and the occasional persistent individual — not by the ordinary taxpaying citizen who has the most direct claim to use it.

Ramesh has paid taxes for thirty years. He has funded every drain, every streetlight, every footpath repair budget in every ward he has ever lived in. He has the standing — the moral standing, the legal standing, the financial standing — to ask exactly where that money went. He has always had it. He has simply never used it.

The shareholder does not wait for the annual report to be sent to them. The shareholder asks for it.

Silence is the luxury of the evader. **Voice is the privilege of the payer.** The evader must stay quiet to avoid the spotlight. The taxpayer can stand in the brightest light and demand accountability — because their name is in the ledger, their money is in the system, and their claim is legitimate in a way that no amount of indignation without contribution can replicate.

What the Voice Sounds Like

It does not sound like anger. Anger is cheap and dismissible. It sounds like precision. It sounds like: I filed an RTI last month. It sounds like: the allocated amount was released in November. It sounds like: I would like to know where that money went.

Ramesh stays for the rest of the meeting. When the drain comes up again, he speaks. Not dramatically. He says: the drainage maintenance budget for this ward is a matter of public record. I am happy to file an RTI on this specific item if the ward office cannot provide an update today. He says it the way he would say anything factual and verifiable. Because it is factual and verifiable.

The official looks at him for a moment. Then he says: we will have an update by next month meeting.

It is not a resolution. But it is not a nod and a register entry either. Something has shifted in the room, fractionally but genuinely. The voice of someone who has paid for the drain is slightly harder to dismiss than the voice of someone who is simply inconvenienced by it.

Ramesh walks out of the meeting into the Sunday afternoon street. He has not fixed the drain. But he has done something he has not done in thirty years of being a taxpayer: he has shown up as one.

5. The Shareholder in Conversation — What to Say at the Dinner Table

Two weeks later, Ramesh is at a family dinner. His brother-in-law Vinay is there — the same Vinay who has been in the same role for twelve years, who spends his Sunday evenings in comfortable stagnation, who has the periodic bad habit of expressing strong opinions about national governance while contributing minimally to the national treasury.

After dinner, over chai, Vinay says what Vinay always says: I do not understand why they do not fix the roads. All this money the government collects and the roads are still a disaster. Where does it all go?

Ramesh has heard this a hundred times. For a hundred times, he has said nothing, or agreed vaguely, or changed the subject. Tonight he does not.

He says, quietly: how much did you pay in income tax last year, Vinay?

Vinay looks mildly affronted. That is personal.

Ramesh nods. Fair enough. I paid roughly one lakh eighty thousand. That is my contribution to the road fund, among other things. When the road is bad, I have specific standing to complain — I have a receipt. I have filed RTIs. I show up to ward meetings. That is what the standing looks like in practice.

He pauses. Then: the system is imperfect. Some of the money is wasted, some is misallocated, some disappears into gaps that should not exist. All of that is worth fighting. But the fight belongs to the people in the system, contributing to it, demanding accountability from inside it. Not to the people watching from outside and commentating.

Vinay is quiet for a moment. Then he says: you sound like a government advertisement.

Ramesh smiles. I sound like someone who has paid for the road and wants it fixed.

The Argument You Will Hear and What It Actually Means

Every honest taxpayer will encounter, at some point, the person who uses national frustration as justification for personal non-contribution. The argument takes many forms but always has the same structure: the system is broken, therefore my contribution to it is optional.

The response is not an argument about the system. The system is imperfect — that is not in dispute and should not be disputed. The response is about standing. About who has the right to demand the repair.

The person who contributes and then demands accountability is exercising a right they have earned. **The person who withholds contribution and then complains about outcomes is a free rider criticising a vehicle they refused to fuel.** These are not morally equivalent positions. And the honest taxpayer does not need to pretend they are.

You do not need to win this argument at every dinner table. You do not need to convert Vinay on a Tuesday evening over chai. But you do not need to go quiet either. The shareholder has the loudest voice in the room — not because they shout, but because their voice is backed by something real.

6. The Receipt in the Concrete — What Ramesh Sees on the Drive Home

It is a Wednesday evening three weeks later. Ramesh is driving home from the office, taking the longer route because the direct road is jammed at this hour. He crosses the new flyover — the one that was under construction for two years, the one everyone complained about, the one that opened eight months ago and quietly made the morning commute forty minutes shorter for everyone in this part of the city.

He has crossed it dozens of times since it opened. He has never particularly thought about it.

Tonight, for some reason, he does.

He thinks about the budget allocation that funded it. He thinks about the tax pool that fed that allocation — the TDS columns of millions of Rameshs across the country, deducted before the salary hit the account, invisible, automatic, unconsented and yet real. He thinks about his own contribution: thirty years, roughly one lakh eighty thousand per year in recent years, smaller amounts in the earlier years when his salary was smaller. A cumulative number that, if he sat down to calculate it, would be substantial.

He thinks: I built this. Not alone. But my name is in it, even if it is invisible. My money is in the concrete. My TDS deduction from April 2009 is somewhere in the steel reinforcement of this flyover, in the salary of an engineer who designed it, in the procurement of the materials that went into it.

He does not feel like a victim. He does not feel like a subject who was taxed to fund something the government decided to build. He feels like a landlord — the quiet satisfaction of someone who invested in a property and can see the investment standing.

The Infrastructure Around You Is Yours

Look around you on any given day in an Indian city. The metro line that moved a million people today. The satellite that makes the GPS in your phone accurate enough to navigate an unfamiliar lane. The mid-day meal that a child in a government school in a district you have never visited ate this morning. The defense installation that you will never see, staffed by soldiers you will never meet, protecting a border you will never need to approach.

None of it arrived by accident. All of it was funded. And a portion of the funding — small in the aggregate, significant in the accumulation — came from the honest declarations of the people who chose the sunlight economy over the shadow one.

The honest taxpayer does not see this clearly because the connection between the TDS column and the flyover is invisible by design — the money passes through institutions, through budgets, through procurement processes, through layers of governance before it becomes concrete. But the connection is real. **The receipt exists. It is printed on the country.**

This is what the shareholder identity ultimately means. Not a formal legal relationship. Not a contractual entitlement. A recognition — quiet, personal, and earned — that the country you live in, with all its imperfections and all its genuine achievements, is partly yours because you helped pay for it. And that recognition changes how you stand in it.

You stop being a guest in your own country. You start being a resident who owns a stake in the building.

And the Building Is Not Finished

Ramesh crosses the flyover. He merges back into the city traffic. Ahead of him, through the windscreen, the skyline of the city he was born in rises against the evening sky — familiar, imperfect, alive with construction cranes and half-finished towers and the particular energy of a place that is still becoming what it intends to be.

He thinks of Arjun. Twenty-six years old, currently in Singapore for a conference, sending back photos of a skyline that looks the way Mumbai might look in twenty years if enough people choose the right things in the next fifteen.

He thinks of Priya. Twenty-five, first ITR filed, first deposit made in the ledger of the Republic.

He thinks of Vikram, filing his response to the show-cause notice on another Sunday morning, staying formal through the exhaustion because the credential to demand better belongs only to the people still inside the system.

He thinks of all the people whose names he will never know — the Rameshs in other cities, other income brackets, other professions — who made the same quiet decision he made thirty years ago and has kept making every year since: to stay in the sunlight, to declare honestly, to contribute fully, and to hold the line.

The infrastructure around him is the sum of those decisions. Not just the flyover. The whole country — the functional parts of it, the parts that work, the parts that are getting better — is the compounded interest on thirty years of people choosing to show up.

He does not know Arjun's question yet. He will hear it soon, when Arjun calls from a rooftop in Singapore, looking at a skyline that India does not yet have and asking why. **But Ramesh already knows part of the answer.**

The skyline you want is the skyline you pay for.

And the payment — honest, full, and without waiting for someone else to go first — is the only thing that has ever built one.

Your tax is your stake in the country. Claim it. Use it. Demand the return.

— ❖ —

Chapter 14
The Global Indian

Competing on an Even Playing Field

Ramesh's younger brother, Arjun, is twenty-six, a brilliant software architect, and is currently travelling abroad for his first major international business conference in Singapore. Ramesh stands at the viewing gallery of Mumbai's Terminal 2, watching the gleaming tail of the aircraft disappear into the night sky. He is proud, but he is also pensive.

When Arjun lands at Changi Airport, he sends a flurry of messages. "Bhaiya, it's incredible. I was out of the plane, through immigration, and in a taxi in exactly twelve minutes. The immigration officer did not even ask to see my return ticket. They just scanned my thumbprint and smiled."

But three days later, the tone of Arjun's messages changes. He is at the conference, networking with peers from Estonia, South Korea, and Germany. He notices a subtle, uncomfortable Standard gap. When the Estonian delegate mentions his country, people think of Digital Nomad Visas and a 100 percent paperless government. When the German speaks, they think of Engineering Precision.

When Arjun speaks, he is greeted with respect for his individual brilliance — but there is always a But. "You Indians are so smart, but why is your infrastructure so messy?" "Your companies are great, but why is it so hard to get a business visa for India?"

Arjun calls Ramesh from a rooftop bar overlooking the Marina Bay Sands. "Bhaiya, why does it feel like we are always playing catch-up? We have the smartest engineers and the hardest workers. Why does an Indian professional have to work twice as hard to prove they are equal to a European or a Singaporean? Why is my passport a burden while theirs is a wing?"

Ramesh realises that what Arjun is feeling is the Sovereign Discount. When a country's collective systems — funded by the discipline of its taxpayers — are weak, every individual citizen carries the weight of that weakness. To be a Global Indian, you need a Global India. And a Global India cannot be built by a population that celebrates settling for less.

1. THE COST OF A WEAK PASSPORT — THE GLOBAL INEFFICIENCY TAX

A passport is more than a travel document. It is the Financial KYC — Know Your Customer — of an entire nation. Countries with high tax-to-GDP ratios and high institutional transparency usually have the strongest passports, with their citizens travelling to 180 or more countries visa-free. The world trusts their systems.

The international community knows that a citizen from a high-compliance nation like Japan or Singapore has a clear financial trail, a stable tax record, and a vested interest in returning home. They are not seen as migration risks or economic fugitives.

Factor	High-Compliance Nation (Japan / Singapore)	Low-Compliance Nation (Shadow Economy Default)
Tax-to-GDP Ratio	30–40% — wide, deep tax base	~11% — narrow funnel, large shadow economy
World's Perception	Clear financial trail, stable record, vested interest in returning home	Potential migration risk, assumed to be hiding something
Passport Strength	180+ countries visa-free — a wing	Visa fees, proof-of-funds queues, weeks of waiting — a burden
Who bears the cost?	**Nobody — honesty is its own dividend**	**Arjun — Rs. 15,000 per visa, 3 days of paperwork, lost career mobility**

By increasing national tax compliance and building a transparent white economy, India is essentially buying a stronger passport for the next generation. The Pullers — those who stay in the cash economy — are the reason the world views our passport with suspicion. Because millions of Indians hide their income, the world assumes every Indian might be hiding something. The non-payer is literally slowing down Arjun's career growth by making his global mobility difficult.

2. THE PRODUCTIVITY GAP — THE 1:5 RATIO AND THE NATIONAL OS

In the global market, talent is a global commodity. Arjun is competing for the same project as a coder in Oslo or a designer in San Francisco. However, there is a hidden factor that determines who wins: Systemic Productivity.

Imagine two identical Ferraris. One is driving on a smooth German Autobahn. The other is driving through a waterlogged, potholed street in a monsoon-hit Indian suburb. Which car reaches the destination first? The speed of the car is irrelevant if the Operating System — the road — is broken. Data shows that a worker in a highly developed, high-tax nation is often 4 to 5 times more productive than an average Indian worker. This is not because they have higher IQs. It is because their National OS is faster.

What Arjun Loses Daily	The Root Cause	The Tax Connection
2 hours in traffic	No Metro built ten years ago — insufficient tax revenue	Every non-payer who avoided tax then is costing Arjun hours today

1 hour in a power outage	Underinvested grid — capital was frozen in gold lockers and cash boxes	Shadow economy capital that never circulated never built the infrastructure
1 hour on slow government portals	Underdigitised public services — digital upgrades require consistent budget allocation	Compliance funds the National OS upgrade that allows Arjun to work, not survive
Total: 4 hours lost per day	A worker in a high-tax developed nation loses none of these hours	**The 1:5 productivity gap is not a talent gap. It is an infrastructure gap.**

When Ramesh pays his tax, he is funding a Software Upgrade for the nation — allowing Arjun to spend 8 hours working instead of 4 hours surviving and 4 hours working. The Lazy Group that settles for Chalta Hai infrastructure is essentially sabotaging the productivity of our best minds. They are keeping the Ferrari in the mud.

3. THE BRAND INDIA PREMIUM — FROM BACK OFFICE TO BOARDROOM

In international business, there is a powerful psychological force called the Country of Origin Effect. It determines what premium the world places on your work before you even open your mouth.

Country of Origin	World's Association	What Built That Premium
Germany	Precision engineering — you pay a premium for a German car	Decades of taxpayer-funded world-class infrastructure, R&D investment, and institutional trust
Switzerland	Reliability — you pay a premium for a Swiss watch	High institutional transparency, funded by one of the world's most compliant tax cultures
India (Today)	Low cost — the world still often expects "Back Office" rates for Indian work	Shadow economy keeps institutional trust low — the brand cannot command a premium
India (The Goal)	**Innovation — Made in India commands R&D Lab rates, not Back Office rates**	**Every honest taxpayer demanding world-class cities is building the Brand India premium**

We want to move from being the World's Back Office — where we do the boring work cheaply — to being the World's R&D Lab — where we do the brilliant work at a premium. But high-value brands are not built in a vacuum. They are built on the Quality of Life. Global talent — the best scientists, researchers, and venture capitalists — only congregates in places where the air is breathable, the schools are world-class, and the legal systems are transparent.

When the Rameshs of India pay their taxes and demand world-class cities, they are building the Global Brand of India. The Puller who hides his income is a Brand Saboteur. He wants Brand India to succeed so he can profit from it — but he refuses to pay for the infrastructure that builds it. He is a Counterfeit Citizen.

4. CAPITAL MAGNETISM — WHY THE WORLD INVESTS IN HONESTY

For decades, India has suffered from Capital Flight. Wealthy Indians, fearful of systemic instability or Inspector Raj, moved their money to tax havens or bought luxury penthouses in Dubai and London. They sought stability elsewhere.

But the world is changing. With global agreements like the Common Reporting Standard and the crackdown on Shell Companies, the shadows are disappearing. The safe havens are closing their doors.

In this new transparent world, the winners will be the Capital Magnets. A country with a wide tax base and a compliant middle class is a Low-Risk Destination. When a global pension fund looks to invest ten billion dollars, it does not look for clever tax evaders. It looks for a nation with Predictable Revenue.

By being an honest taxpayer, Ramesh is signalling to global markets that India is a safe, mature, and transparent place to invest. This brings in Foreign Direct Investment — the only mechanism that creates the millions of high-paying jobs the next generation needs. The non-payer, by keeping the economy grey, makes India look risky — which keeps interest rates high and foreign investment low.

5. SOVEREIGN DEBT — RAMESH AS A RATING AGENCY

India's tax-to-GDP ratio of approximately 11 percent is a stark contrast to the OECD average of approximately 34 percent. On the global stage, this ratio is our Credit Score — and a low score means India pays a higher premium on every rupee it borrows internationally.

Scenario	What Happens to India's Rating	What That Unlocks
Tax compliance jumps 5% — more Rameshs, fewer Pullers	Sovereign Credit Rating climbs meaningfully toward investment-grade A levels	Billions saved in bond interest — money that stays in India to build IITs, AIIMS hospitals, and high-speed rail

Tax compliance stagnates — Pullers stay in the shadow economy	India rated just above Junk — government pays high Risk Premium on every global bond	Interest payments consume one in four budget rupees — no money left for the infrastructure Arjun needs
FDI flows into a wide-tax-base, compliant economy	Global pension funds and sovereign wealth funds see India as Low-Risk, predictable	Millions of high-paying jobs created for the next generation — Arjun's children compete on equal terms globally

That saved interest is money that does not leave our shores. It is money that stays in India to build new IITs, new AIIMS hospitals, and high-speed rail corridors that connect our villages to our ports.

Ramesh is the Rating Agency. Every time he chooses to file an honest return, he is upgrading India's global credit score. Every time a Puller hides their income, they are downgrading the nation's future.

6. THE NEW INDIAN PATRIOTISM — ECONOMIC EXCELLENCE

In the 20th century, patriotism was defined by the willingness to defend the border — a physical, martial duty. In the 21st century, patriotism is defined by Economic Excellence.

Century	How Patriotism Was Defined	What It Required
20th Century	Willingness to defend the border — physical, martial duty	Courage, sacrifice, and the soldier at the frontier
21st Century	**Economic Excellence — your personal productivity is national service**	**An honest ITR, an ambitious career, and the demand for accountability from the systems you fund**

Being a Global Indian means realising that your personal success is inextricably linked to your country's reputation. You cannot be a billionaire in a poor country and expect the world's respect. True respect — the kind that gets you visa-free entry and a seat at the G7 table — comes when you lead a nation that is self-reliant, transparent, and built on the contributions of its own people.

The Lazy Majority that settles for less, avoids the tax net, and hacks the system is not just avoiding a payment. They are Economic Saboteurs. They are the reason an Indian professional has to stand in a longer queue. They are the reason our Operating System is slow.

7. THE OAR AND THE OCEAN

Ramesh looks at his phone. Arjun has sent a photo of the Singapore skyline. It is beautiful, efficient, and expensive.

Ramesh types back: "Arjun, look at those buildings. Every brick was paid for by a citizen who believed that their personal growth depended on their national growth. Do not just admire their city — help me build ours. The speed at which you move forward in that international queue depends on how many of us at home are willing to pick up the oar and pay for the path."

Ramesh's tax is not just a domestic transaction. It is an International Investment. It is his way of ensuring that when Arjun stands at a counter in London or New York five years from now, the officer does not see a Risk. They see a Partner. They see a Global Indian from a Global India.

The Free Ride is a myth. The Global India is a subscription. And it is time we all paid our dues.

— ❖ —

Chapter 15
The Receipt

Dear Ramesh

A Letter to the Invisible Hero

1. The Letter Nobody Sent

Every year, somewhere between the last week of March and the first week of April, a quiet ritual takes place across India. It happens in kitchens before dawn, at office desks during lunch breaks, on phones in the back seats of autos, and in the glow of laptop screens late at night. It is the ritual of tax filing — the annual act of accounting for oneself to the nation.

It involves gathering documents that nobody enjoys gathering: Form 16s and bank statements, rent receipts and investment proofs, premium certificates and challan numbers. It involves navigating portals that crash at peak traffic. It involves, for many, a visit to a CA who will charge a fee to perform the act of honesty that the system has made too complicated to perform alone.

And when it is done — when the return is filed, the acknowledgment number is generated, and the small digital confirmation arrives — there is no ceremony. No recognition. No acknowledgment from the state that has just received, once again, the contribution of one of its most reliable and essential citizens.

The acknowledgment number is not a thank you. It is a receipt for a transaction. It says: we have received your filing. It does not say: we see you. It does not say: we know what this cost you. It does not say: we understand that the number on that form represents years of disciplined work, of deferred pleasures, of quiet sacrifices made in the name of a social contract you chose to honor — even when honoring it was inconvenient, even when others around you were choosing not to.

This chapter is the letter that acknowledgment number never was.

This chapter is for you, Ramesh. And for every person in this country who is, in any meaningful sense, a Ramesh.

2. Let Us See You — Fully, Finally

You are the person who checks the salary slip every month, finds the TDS column, and feels the familiar pull of resignation mixed with something quieter — a kind of dignity in accepting what is required of you.

You are the person who, when the office canteen conversation turns to "smart" tax arrangements — cash deals, undeclared rent, income routed through relatives — smiles politely and says nothing, because the truth is too complicated to explain in a lunch break. The truth being: you don't do those things. Not because you haven't thought about them. Not because the temptation has never formed. But because somewhere in your personal accounting of who you are, the cost of those shortcuts is higher than their price.

You are not naive. You are not unaware of what others do. You are simply unwilling to be the kind of person who does it.

You are the person who goes to the government hospital with your father and feels a complex mixture of frustration at the queue and something approaching pride at the new equipment in the diagnostic room — because you know, in the private ledger of your conscience, that you helped pay for that machine.

You are the person who uses the flyover that everyone complained about during construction and nobody remembers the complaints about now. You are the person who watches the Vande Bharat train speed past on the news and does not say "the government built that." You say — quietly, privately, to no one in particular — "we built that."

You are the backbone of the Indian Republic. You have always been. This book has spent fourteen chapters making the argument. This chapter simply wants to look you in the eye and say: **we know. We see you. You have been seen all along** — even when the system made you feel invisible.

3. What You Actually Built — The Full Receipt

You have asked, at various points in your life, where your money goes. You have stood at the TDS column and wondered whether any of it makes a difference. You have felt the vertigo of paying for a system that sometimes seems indifferent to your existence.

So let us give you the receipt that the acknowledgment number never did.

Every time Ramesh paid his taxes — every month, every year, for his entire working life — something was built. Not all of it was visible. Not all of it was efficient. Some of it was wasted, and that waste is real and deserves to be fought. But the sum of what was built is staggering, and it belongs to you as much as to anyone who cut a ribbon in front of it.

The roads that connect the village your parents came from to the city where you built your career — you built those. Not alone. But your contribution is in the concrete.

The satellites that ISRO launches, that make the GPS in your phone accurate enough to navigate an unfamiliar city — you funded the scientists who designed them. Your tax paid their salaries on the months when the budget was tight and the mission was uncertain.

The mid-day meal that a child in a government school in a district you have never visited ate this morning — that meal exists partly because you paid your TDS without being asked twice.

The soldier standing at a post in conditions you will thankfully never experience, protecting a border you will thankfully never need to approach — his uniform, his training, his equipment, and his salary are partly a product of your contribution. You bought his boots. Chapter 1 said this. It remains true in Chapter 15.

The vaccination that reached 800 million people during a pandemic that could have destroyed this country's social fabric — you pre-paid for that vaccine. It felt free to the person who received it. To you it was a prepaid insurance premium, paid monthly, for decades, in the form of a deduction you never got to approve.

The digital infrastructure that lets a street vendor in Varanasi accept a UPI payment on a phone — infrastructure that other countries pay private corporations billions to maintain — was built with public money. Your money. The money that left your account before it reached your hands.

This is your receipt. It is not printed on paper. **It is printed on the country.**

4. To the Preethi in Every Reader

This book introduced you to Preethi in Chapter 7. Thirty-two years old. Senior Manager in Bengaluru. Self-made in every dimension of that word. She had built a fortress of entirely understandable justifications around one small act of non-declaration — and then, on a quiet Friday morning with a cup of coffee and an honest conversation, she chose to take the fortress down.

She did it in eleven minutes. She did it alone. Nobody forced her. Nobody watched. Nobody rewarded her for it.

She did it because she understood something that this book has tried to articulate from the very first page: that honesty in a system is not a gift you give the government. It is an investment you make in yourself. In your financial identity. In your legal standing. In your moral authority to demand that the system serve you as well as you have served it.

If you are Preethi — if you are reading this and recognizing in her story the outline of your own quiet arrangements — this chapter is not asking you to feel guilty. Guilt is not useful here. What is useful is clarity.

You are too capable, too principled, and too important to this country's future to spend any portion of your considerable intelligence building fortresses around a decision that does not reflect who you actually are. You fought for your seat at every table you now occupy. You declared your ambition and demanded to be paid for it. You built your financial independence with your own hands. **The formal economy is not your adversary. It is your infrastructure.** Come back to it fully. Not because the system deserves it. Because you do.

5. To the Akash in Every Reader

Akash appeared in Chapter 4, sitting in Silk Board traffic, looking at his payslip, calling his brother to ask why success feels like punishment. His ₹4.5 lakh annual tax deduction felt like a theft — money taken before he could decide what to do with it, by a government he hadn't voted to trust with his bonus.

By the end of that chapter he understood something important: that he did not build his career in a vacuum. That the India Stack, the legal system, the IIT or NIT that educated him at a fraction of its real cost, the stability that allowed venture capital to flow into the startup ecosystem that created his job — all of it was funded by the collective contribution of people like him, and people who came before him.

He went to work the next morning feeling like a Sovereign instead of a victim. Not because his tax bill shrank. Because his understanding of what it bought had grown.

If you are Akash — if you are the high-earning professional who feels the 30% bracket as a personal injustice — this is the reminder: **you are not being taxed for your success.** You are being recognized as someone with the capacity to fund the conditions that made your success possible. That is not punishment. That is the highest form of civic trust. Carry it accordingly.

6. To the Vinay in Every Reader

Vinay is the hardest person to write this section for. Because Vinay is comfortable, and comfort is not a crime. He waters his plants. He loves his family. He is kind to his neighbors. He is, by most ordinary measures, a good man.

But this book has argued — carefully, with data, with consequence, and with as much compassion as the argument allows — that comfort at the level of national contribution is not a private choice. It ripples outward. It arrives, years later, in overcrowded hospitals and underfunded schools and daughters who cannot afford apartments in cities their parents helped build by other means.

If you are Vinay — if you recognize in his Sunday evening the outline of your own settled contentment — this chapter is not asking you to become someone you are not. It is asking you to become **more fully who you already are.** You are not a person without potential. You are a person who has not yet been given a compelling enough reason to deploy it.

Here is the reason: India's demographic window is closing. The generation that can still change the trajectory is yours. The taxpayers of tomorrow are the ambitious citizens of today. The nation you will grow old in is being built right now, by whoever chooses to build it.

Comfort is a beautiful destination. Make sure you have earned it before you arrive.

7. To the Vicky and the Gupta Ji in Every Reader

This book has not been easy on you.

It has called you a Puller. It has put you in tables with red cells. It has described your Sunday morning freedom as a tax on someone else's ambition, your cash transaction as a vote against Priya's future, your comfortable invisibility as an anchor on the boat.

That was necessary. The arithmetic is real. The consequences are real. And a book that softened that truth would have been less honest than the citizens it is asking you to become.

But this section is not the arithmetic. This section is the door.

Because here is what the book has not yet said directly to you: it understands why you are where you are. The system was not designed to welcome you. It was designed, for most of its history, to frighten you — to make compliance feel like walking into a room where everyone assumes you have done something wrong. The forms were impenetrable. The portals crashed. The notices arrived for reasons you could not decipher, demanding responses in a language that required a paid translator. The honest man down the street did not seem to be living noticeably better than you. The incentive to step into the sunlight was invisible. The cost of staying in the shadow was, for a long time, close to zero.

You were not wrong to read that environment the way you read it. You were rational.

But the environment has changed. The new Income Tax Act has 536 sections where there were 819. It is written in language a non-specialist can read. The portal pre-fills most of what you need to declare. The threshold below which you owe nothing at all has risen to Rs. 12 lakhs — meaning the first step into the formal economy, for most small earners, costs nothing except the act of showing up. The shadows are shrinking not because enforcement has become fiercer, though it has, but because the sunlight has become genuinely warmer.

And the sunlight gives you things the shadow never could. It gives you a credit history. It gives you a loan at a rate a moneylender will never offer. It gives you the financial identity that means a bank sees a person with a story, not a person with nothing on paper. It gives you the standing — the moral, legal, documented standing — to demand that the road outside your shop gets fixed, that the school your children attend gets a proper teacher, that the system that has historically ignored you begins, finally, to see you.

The shadow economy promised you freedom. What it gave you was smallness.

You do not have to stay small.

The door to the formal economy is open. It has always been open. It is more open now than it has ever been in the sixty years since Independence. You do not need to walk through it perfectly. You do not need to arrive with thirty years of clean filings and a spotless record. You need only to begin — one return, one invoice, one declared rupee — and let the compounding of honest contribution do what it has always done for the Rameshs who chose it before you.

The boat has room for more rowers. The oar is not heavy on the first day. And the shore — the ten trillion dollar India, the country where Priya can afford her apartment and the hospital has the equipment and the road outside your shop does not flood every monsoon — that shore gets closer every time someone new picks up the oar.

You do not need to have been a Ramesh from the beginning. You only need to decide to become one now.

8. What Ramesh Knows Now That He Did Not Know at the Beginning

We began this book on a Mumbai local train. Ramesh's phone buzzing. The SMS from his bank: Salary Credited. His thumb lingering on the TDS column. ₹12,500. Gone. The Kashmir trip. The sunburst guitar. His daughter's coaching classes. His father's medicine.

He felt it then as loss. As the silent, unconsenting extraction of what was rightfully his.

Fourteen chapters later, Ramesh is still on that train. The TDS column still shows ₹12,500. The deduction has not changed. The system has not been perfected. The potholes outside his building are — let us be honest — still there.

But something has changed. Not in the system. In Ramesh.

He no longer looks at that number and feels only loss. He looks at it and feels the weight of what it represents — not the weight of a burden, but the weight of a contribution. The weight of matter, of presence, of consequence. The weight of a person who exists in the formal record of a nation and whose existence in that record is not nothing. It is, in fact, everything.

He knows now that the ₹12,500 is not gone. It has been transformed. Into a brick somewhere. Into a salary somewhere. Into a meal somewhere. Into a child's chance somewhere. The transformation is imperfect and the system through which it travels is flawed. But the transformation is real.

He knows now that he is not a passenger in this country. He is not a guest. He is not a subject receiving whatever the state decides to distribute. **He is a shareholder. A primary funder. An architect of the only India that will ever exist in his lifetime and his daughter's lifetime.**

He knows that the people who opt out — the shadow economy dwellers, the comfort zone settlers, the fortress builders — are not his enemies. They are his fellow citizens who have not yet arrived at the understanding he has arrived at. Some of them will. Some of them are reading this book right now.

And he knows that his job is not to resent them. His job is to keep rowing. To keep contributing. To keep demanding — loudly, morally, with the full authority of someone who has paid their share — that the system improve, that the potholes get fixed, that the hospitals get funded, that the schools get teachers, that the satellite gets launched.

He has earned that voice. It cost him ₹12,500 a month for thirty years. **It is the most powerful voice in the Republic.**

9. Priya — The Person This Was All For

There is one more person in this book who has not yet had her moment in the final chapter. She has appeared in glimpses — asleep in her room while Ramesh made promises, asking questions in hospital waiting rooms, filing her own returns with the same meticulous honesty her father taught her.

She is Priya. And she is the answer to every question this book has asked.

Every argument for honest taxpaying ultimately comes back to a child — to the generation that inherits whatever this one builds or fails to build. To the person who will one day stand at a salary slip of their own and feel the pull of the TDS column and have to decide, in that moment, what kind of citizen they intend to be.

Priya did not choose to be born into a country with an 11% Tax-to-GDP ratio. She did not choose the shadow economy that inflated the property prices that made her apartment search difficult. She did not choose the comfortable stagnation of the Vinays that narrowed the tax base that underfunded the hospitals she waited in.

But she chose — every month, without fail, with the same quiet resolution her father modeled for her — to pay her full share. To stand in the sunlight of the formal economy. To be visible, contributing, present.

She does it not because she is naive about the system's flaws. She is not. She has lived them. She does it because she understands something her father spent a lifetime learning and this book has spent fifteen chapters arguing:

The country does not belong to those who consume it. It belongs to those who build it. And building it means paying for it — honestly, fully, and without waiting for someone else to go first.

She is the first person in her family to earn more than her father did at her age. She is the first woman in her extended family to own property in her own name. She is, in the language of this book, a Pusher — a rower, a contributor, a load-bearing column of the Republic.

She is also, quietly and without drama, the most important person in this story. Because everything Ramesh did — every month of TDS, every filed return, every honest declaration, every pothole he absorbed and every accountability he demanded — was, at its deepest level, an act performed in the direction of her future.

He did not do it for the government. He did not do it for the economists or the policy papers or the GDP charts. He did it so that the country Priya inherited would be slightly more functional, slightly more honest, slightly more capable of rewarding the effort of people who choose to engage with it fully.

He did it because he loved her. And because loving someone, in the largest sense, means **caring about the world they will have to live in after you are gone.**

10. The Taxpayer's Creed — The Final Version

In Chapter 13 this book offered a Taxpayer's Creed — five declarations for the citizen who has chosen to be a shareholder rather than a subject. This chapter offers one final version. Not a list this time. A single paragraph. The distillation of everything that came before.

I am a citizen of the Indian Republic. I work hard, I earn honestly, and I contribute fully —

not because the system is perfect, not because I have been asked nicely, and not because

I expect a thank you that will likely never come. I contribute because I understand something

that cannot be unlearned once it is learned: that the country I want is the country I pay for,

and the future I hope my children inherit is the future I am building right now,

one honest declaration at a time. I am not a victim of this system.

I am its primary funder, its most essential citizen, and its most powerful voice

for accountability and reform. I am the backbone of the Indian Republic.

And backbones do not break.

11. The Acknowledgment Number — Rewritten

When your tax filing is complete this year, you will receive an acknowledgment number. It will be a long string of digits that means nothing emotionally and everything administratively. It will confirm that your filing has been received.

But read it differently this time.

Read it as the receipt for something larger than a financial transaction. Read it as proof that you showed up. That you were counted. That you chose the sunlight over the shadow, the formal over the informal, the contributing over the consuming.

Read it as the receipt for the road that connected a village to a city. For the vaccine that reached a family that could not have afforded it otherwise. For the satellite that a scientist spent years designing on a government salary that your tax helped pay. For the soldier's boots. For the child's mid-day meal. For the diagnostic machine in the government hospital that your father used last year.

Read it as the receipt for Priya's future.

And then put it away, go back to your life, and keep rowing.

Because the boat is still moving. The shore is closer than it has ever been. And it is moving because of you.

Pay with Pride. Demand with Power. Build with Passion.

— For every Ramesh, everywhere. —

— ❖ —

The Salaried Indian

Data Reference Table — All 55 Data Points

Sl.	Data Point Used in Book	Page(s)	Reference / Source
1	1.4 billion — India's population	pp. 2, 6, 13, 17, 18, 26, 30, 33, 69, 131, 141	Office of the Registrar General & Census Commissioner, India — Census 2011 projections; United Nations World Population Prospects 2022.
2	8.2 crore people filed ITRs in the last assessment year	p.3	Income Tax Department, Govt. of India — CBDT Annual Report 2023-24; CBDT press release on ITR filing statistics, AY 2023-24.
3	Less than 3% of India's population pays personal income tax	pp. 3, 20, 26	Derived from CBDT ITR data (8.2 crore filers) vs. projected population 140 crore. Cited in Economic Times, Mint, Business Standard (2023-24).

Sl.	Data Point Used in Book	Page(s)	Reference / Source
4	Rs. 19.58 lakh crore — gross Direct Tax collections (record)	p.3	CBDT Press Release, Ministry of Finance — Gross Direct Tax Collections FY 2023-24 (advance estimates); PIB India, March 2024.
5	Personal Income Tax exceeds Corporate Tax — second consecutive year	p.3	CBDT Annual Report 2023-24; Union Budget 2024-25 receipts budget. Reported: Hindu BusinessLine and Mint, July 2024.
6	India's informal sector: 40–45% of GDP; shadow economy: 20–45% of GDP	pp. 4, 10, 61	IMF Working Paper WP/22/256 "Informality and the Shadow Economy in India"; ILO World Employment and Social Outlook 2023; NCAER estimates.
7	90% of India's workforce is in the informal sector	p.10	ILO Employment Report 2023 — India Chapter; National Sample Survey (NSS) 68th Round; Economic Survey 2022-23, Ministry of Finance.
8	India median age ~28; 65%+ of population is working-age (15–64)	pp. 11, 79, 80	UNFPA India Ageing Report 2023; UN World Population Prospects 2022; Census India demographic projections.

Sl.	Data Point Used in Book	Page(s)	Reference / Source
9	Demographic window closes ~2040 — dependency ratio begins rising	pp. 12, 79	UN World Population Prospects 2022 (India dependency ratio projections); UNFPA India; Economic Survey 2022-23.
10	Per-capita GDP ~$2,700 (current); $10,000 target for Developed Nation status	p.9	World Bank Open Data — India GDP per capita (US$), 2023; IMF World Economic Outlook 2024; standard development economics threshold.
11	220 crore COVID-19 doses delivered; 80 crore received free food (PMGKAY)	p.15	CoWIN Dashboard, Ministry of Health & Family Welfare; Ministry of Consumer Affairs — PMGKAY beneficiary data 2020-23; PIB press releases.
12	UPI processed over 131 billion transactions in last fiscal year	pp. 16, 25, 106	National Payments Corporation of India (NPCI) Annual Report 2023-24; NPCI UPI Product Statistics (monthly releases, FY 2023-24).
13	Rs. 2.5 lakh crore — govt annual spend on power and renewable energy	p.16	Union Budget 2024-25, Ministry of Finance — Expenditure Budget, Dept. of Energy; Ministry of New & Renewable Energy Annual Report 2023-24.

Sl.	Data Point Used in Book	Page(s)	Reference / Source
14	Rs. 11.11 lakh crore — Capital Expenditure (Union Budget 2024-25)	pp.16,22	Union Budget 2024-25, Ministry of Finance — Budget at a Glance; Expenditure Profile 2024-25.
15	Rs. 6.21 lakh crore — Defence Budget	pp.18,22	Union Budget 2024-25, Ministry of Finance — Defence Services Estimates 2024-25; Ministry of Defence Annual Report 2023-24.
16	~Rs. 11 lakh crore — annual Interest Payments on national debt	p.22	Union Budget 2024-25 — Interest Payments (Major Head 2049); RBI Handbook of Statistics 2023; Medium Term Fiscal Policy Statement 2024-25.
17	Rs. 48 lakh crore — total national budget	p.21	Union Budget 2024-25, Ministry of Finance — Total Expenditure; Budget at a Glance 2024-25.
18	Jal Jeevan Mission: over 75% of rural households now have tap water	p.22	Jal Jeevan Mission Dashboard, Ministry of Jal Shakti (jaljeevanmission.gov.in); PIB — "Har Ghar Jal" coverage update, 2024.

Sl.	Data Point Used in Book	Page(s)	Reference / Source
19	IIT/NIT fees Rs. 8–10 lakh (4 years); actual govt cost per engineer Rs. 35–40 lakh	p.26	CAG Report on Functioning of IITs (2015, updated estimates); Ministry of Education per-student expenditure data; Times of India (2022-23).
20	~6,500 millionaires projected to leave India in 2022	p.28	Henley Private Wealth Migration Report 2022; Financial Express, CNBC TV18, The Economic Times (June 2022).
21	1.69 lakh individuals declared income over Rs. 1 crore — AY 2023-24	p.27	Income Tax Department data AY 2023-24; Lok Sabha Starred/Unstarred Questions on ITR filing statistics; CBDT Annual Report 2023-24.
22	London tax rate: 40–45%; UK GDP growth: 0.5–1%	p.28	HMRC UK Tax Rates & Thresholds 2023-24; UK Office for National Statistics (ONS) GDP growth data 2023; IMF World Economic Outlook 2024.
23	PMGKAY covers 80 crore beneficiaries with free rations	p.33	Ministry of Consumer Affairs, Food & Public Distribution; PIB press release on PMGKAY extension (2023-24). ~81.35 crore beneficiaries.

Sl.	Data Point Used in Book	Page(s)	Reference / Source
24	Corporate tax rate cut from 30% to 22% (existing companies)	p.34	The Taxation Laws (Ordinance) 2019; Section 115BAA of Income Tax Act 1961; Ministry of Finance press release, September 2019.
25	Private school/ coaching fees rising at 10–12% per annum	pp.34,35	FICCI-EY Education Report 2023; ASSOCHAM Education Survey 2022; Mint and Indian Express — private school fee inflation analysis (2019-2023).
26	Healthcare costs rising at ~14% per annum — among highest in Asia	p.35	National Health Accounts (NHA) Estimates for India 2019-20, Ministry of Health; Willis Towers Watson India Healthcare Cost Trend Report 2023.
27	Petrol: effective tax rate exceeds 50% of pump price	p.35	PPAC (Petroleum Planning & Analysis Cell), Ministry of Petroleum — Retail Selling Price breakdown; Central Excise Duty + State VAT, 2023-24.
28	GST rates: laptop 18%, car 28%+cess, restaurant 5–18%, health insurance 18%, AC 28%	pp.19,35	CBIC — GST Rate Schedule (as amended 2023); GST Council decisions; CBIC Tariff Notifications.

Sl.	Data Point Used in Book	Page(s)	Reference / Source
29	India Tax-to-GDP ~11%; OECD average ~34%	pp. 50, 71, 82, 106, 121, 131	OECD Revenue Statistics 2023; IMF Article IV India Consultation 2023; RBI Handbook of Statistics 2023; World Bank WDI 2023.
30	2.2 crore pay meaningful income tax; 30–40% may have undisclosed income; ~Rs. 1 lakh crore hidden annually	p.52	CBDT ITR data cross-referenced with NIPFP estimates; IMF Working Paper on India Tax Gap (2022). Aggregate is author extrapolation — illustrative.
31	India GDP ~$3.7 trillion; 25% shadow economy = ~$925 billion unrecorded annually	p.61	IMF World Economic Outlook April 2024 (India GDP); Schneider, F. (2022) "Shadow Economy Around the World"; IMF WP/22/256.
32	Black money inflates real estate 30–40%; 2-BHK worth Rs. 60 lakh priced at Rs. 1.5 crore	pp.61,72	NHB RESIDEX data; RBI Annual Report — Real Estate Prices; ANAROCK Research Report 2023; Black Money Act 2015 legislative preamble.

Sl.	Data Point Used in Book	Page(s)	Reference / Source
33	Rs. 1.98 lakh crore GST evasion detected by DGGI in 2023	p.61	DGGI Annual Report 2022-23; Ministry of Finance press release on GST evasion detection; PTI and Business Standard reports (2023).
34	Moneylender interest: 2–3%/month (24–36% pa); formal bank SME loan: 9–11%	p.63	RBI Report on Trend & Progress of Banking in India 2022-23 (formal SME lending rates); NABARD Rural Credit Survey (moneylender rates).
35	ITR filers jumped from 3.8 crore to over 8 crore over the past decade	p.66	CBDT Annual Reports 2013-14 through 2023-24; Ministry of Finance data on ITR filing trends. Reported: Economic Times, Business Standard.
36	WHO recommends 1 doctor per 1,000 people; India has ~0.7 per 1,000	p.71	WHO Global Health Observatory — Health Workforce Data (India); National Health Profile 2022, Central Bureau of Health Intelligence, MoHFW.
37	India home loan rate ~9%; OECD nations 3–4%	pp. 71, 72, 132, 136	SBI / HDFC / ICICI published home loan rates (2024); ECB key interest rate data (eurozone); US Fed mortgage rate statistics; RBI MPC Report 2024.

Sl.	Data Point Used in Book	Page(s)	Reference / Source
38	India Sovereign Credit Rating: Baa3/BBB- (few notches above junk); OECD nations A or above	pp. 71, 72, 135, 136	Moody's Investors Service — India Sovereign Rating 2023 (Baa3, stable); S&P Global Ratings India (BBB-, stable); Fitch Ratings India 2023.
39	Denmark/ Singapore shadow economy: below 5–7% of GDP	p. 65	Schneider, Buehn, Montenegro (2022) "Shadow Economies All Over the World." World Bank Policy Research Working Paper; IMF Nordic estimates.
40	Worker productivity: Indian worker 4–5x less productive than in high-tax developed nation	pp. 132, 133	ILO World Employment & Social Outlook 2023 — Labour Productivity; World Bank WDI — Output per worker; McKinsey Global Institute (2020).
41	IT Act 1961: 819+ sections, 47 chapters → IT Act 2025: 536 sections, 23 chapters; effective April 1, 2026	pp. 94, 99, 105	Income Tax Act 2025 (Act No. 25 of 2025); Gazette of India, August 21, 2025; Ministry of Finance press release; PRS Legislative Research.

Sl.	Data Point Used in Book	Page(s)	Reference / Source
42	President gave assent to IT Act 2025 on August 21, 2025	p. 99	Gazette of India Extraordinary, Part II, Section 1, August 21, 2025; Ministry of Finance official notification.
43	Rs. 12 lakh effective zero-tax threshold (after rebates under Section 87A)	pp. 99, 106	Union Budget 2025-26; Finance Bill 2025; CBDT Circular on rebate under Section 87A; Ministry of Finance press release, February 2025.
44	India GDP growth ~7%; potential 9–10% if tax base widens to 60% of OECD levels	p. 54	IMF World Economic Outlook 2024 (India growth ~6.8-7%); IMF Article IV India 2023 (potential output); author extrapolation — illustrative.
45	800 million (80 crore) vaccinated during COVID pandemic	p. 141	CoWIN Dashboard, Ministry of Health & Family Welfare — cumulative vaccination data; WHO India Country Office vaccination reports 2021-22.
46	Petrol tax >50% of pump price (cross-reference)	pp. 19, 35	See Reference 27 above — same source (PPAC data).

Sl.	Data Point Used in Book	Page(s)	Reference / Source
47	Effective total tax burden (direct + indirect) for middle-class: 25–30% of gross income	p. 98	Author calculation: income tax ~15% effective + GST on consumption 10–15% of net income. Consistent with RBI working papers. Illustrative.
48	Suresh contribution ~Rs. 1,200/ month; 1 million Sureshes = Rs. 1,200 crore/ month	p.8	Illustrative calculation: Rs. 30,000 income × 5% effective indirect tax rate on essentials. Author-constructed example.
49	Ramesh contributes Rs. 40,000–45,000/ month; Suresh Rs. 1,200/ month — 33x ratio	pp. 11, 20	Illustrative model: Rs. 1,50,000 income × 15% effective income tax + 18–28% GST on consumption. Consistent with CBDT and CBIC rate structures.
50	Visa/Mastercard transaction fee 2–3% in developed nations; UPI: near-zero	pp. 16, 25	NPCI and RBI data on UPI costs; Visa/Mastercard merchant service charge documentation (USA/EU market). Widely reported in fintech literature.

Sl.	Data Point Used in Book	Page(s)	Reference / Source
51	CBDT penalty authority: up to 200% of disputed tax amount	p. 41	Section 270A of Income Tax Act 1961 (misreporting/ under-reporting of income penalty); CBDT circular on penalty provisions.
52	Tax litigation average resolution time: 12–15 years in India	p. 41	CBDT data on pending appeals and litigation; Income Tax Appellate Tribunal (ITAT) disposal rate studies; PRS Legislative Research (2022).
53	TDS discrepancy notice: Rs. 12,000 demand; Rs. 8,000 CA fee to defend	pp.96, 109	Illustrative figure — based on CBDT data on notices issued (Annual Report 2023-24) and ICAI CA fee estimates. Marked illustrative.
54	Income tax reopening period: up to 7 years for undisclosed income	p.41	Section 148A of Income Tax Act 1961 (as amended by Finance Act 2021); CBDT Instruction No. 1 of 2023 on reopening of assessments.
55	Gupta Ji AI flag: Rs. 4 lakh declared income vs. Rs. 60 lakh SUV — Project Insight	p.66	Income Tax Department — Project Insight (AI/ML compliance initiative); CBDT Annual Report 2022-23 on data analytics enforcement; PIB press release.

www.ingramcontent.com/pod-product-compliance
Lightning Source LLC
LaVergne TN
LVHW100308210926
848480LV00003B/1057
9798904510367